WOODBURNING
WORKSHOP

WOODBURNING
WORKSHOP

Essential Techniques & Creative Projects for Beginners

Court O'Reilly

stashBOOKS®

an imprint of C&T Publishing

THIS BOOK IS DEDICATED TO:

Finnley & Miles.

Let your fiery passions &
burning desires be the fuel
to achieve your goals.

Welcome to Woodburning

WOODBURNING, OR PYROGRAPHY, is the controlled application of a heated object to wood and other materials to create artwork from the burn marks. The word pyrography translates to "writing with fire" from the Greek origin *pur* (fire) and *graphos* (writing). Woodburning has existed since the beginning of recorded history. It was practiced by many cultures, including the Egyptians and some African tribes. With modern technology, we have electric woodburning tools with temperature control settings and interchangeable nibs to burn artwork safely and precisely.

Woodburning has become a popular hobby for people of all ages from different creative backgrounds, including people with no artistic experience. It is a safe hobby that anyone can learn quickly to make customized wooden items. The slow and relaxing process of woodburning makes it highly attractive and therapeutic. Transferring heat from the woodburning tool to burn wood is like no other hobby! ❀

My First Time Woodburning

I first purchased a woodburning tool to burn initials into a canoe paddle. I instantly became hooked when the hot nib started burning the wood, and I could smell the subtle campfire scent and feel the warmth from the tool at my fingertips. I was relaxed, focused, and found joy in creating a custom gift for someone near and dear to me. That quickly snowballed into learning proper woodburning techniques and practicing on different wood items. I found my niche in nature-themed artwork, and eventually, my close family and friends wanted commissioned art pieces. Next thing you know, I am teaching woodburning workshops, taking commissions globally, and writing my own woodburning book!

Everyone is called to woodburning for different reasons, and everyone's woodburning journey is unique. Beginner woodburners end up sticking with the hobby for a multitude of reasons. They might enjoy the sensory experience of burning, expressing themselves through their artwork, experiencing a meditative state when creating, the pleasure of woodburning for friends and family, or the satisfaction of finishing a project. You may pick up the woodburning tool today for one reason and end your session realizing there are so many more reasons your woodburning hobby resonates with you.

The Benefits of Woodburning

Nothing compares to the hobby of woodburning. The use of heat and natural wooden materials creates a peaceful and cozy environment to make art. Whether you are a beginner or transitioning from another craft, woodburning will feel brand new with so much to learn.

You'll soon discover the positive impact woodburning has on your wellbeing. It is a slow process that teaches patience, reduces stress, increases focus, and enhances your creative skills. Many woodburning artists experience the state of flow—a tranquil mental state of being fully conscious of the present moment—while burning. In the flow state, your mind entirely focuses and immerses in the activity at hand. It's not hard to feel grounded and relaxed when your entire focus is on the smell of campfire, warmth from the tool, and natural wood elements while creating art that you connect with.

In addition to being a relaxing hobby, woodburning is relatively inexpensive, with minimal materials required for each project. The setup and cleanup are quick and simple, making it easy to sit down and burn for five minutes or five hours, depending on your schedule. Woodburning is also a conveniently portable hobby. You can pack your tool, wood, and materials into a small bag and take them wherever you go.

You are not limited to woodburning on one type or size of material. There is a huge selection of raw wood products with different shapes, styles, functions, and grain colors. You can woodburn wall art or functional items such as coasters, charcuterie boards, boxes, utensils, centerpieces, signs, and anything else that is wooden and safe to burn. You can even use your woodburning tool to burn on canvas, leather, cork, gourds, bones, paper, and more!

One of my favorite reasons for learning woodburning is the ability to customize art and gifts for others. For holidays and special occasions, personalized woodburning gifts are always well received!

Imperfection is Perfection

The outcome of your final woodburning artwork may look slightly different than the pattern you are referencing. Don't be discouraged if that is the case. Imperfection is perfection when it comes to woodburning art! What you may consider imperfect is what gives your final woodburning artwork character, originality, and rustic charm. No matter how good you are as an artist, no woodburning artwork can be replicated perfectly from a pattern. That is what a laser engraving machine is for!

Woodburning is widely practiced because of the creative process from start to finish. It is the same reason knitters make scarves instead of buying them or woodworkers make furniture instead of buying it. There's a satisfaction in creating and accomplishing that encourages the maker to keep making. It is truly fulfilling to complete a goal you set for yourself and have a piece of artwork that you can call your own at the end of your project.

What to Expect as a Beginner

Here are some things to expect when you first start practicing woodburning. Learning something new can be exciting and challenging. Still, without prior woodburning experience, you may wonder what is normal and what is not when you are starting out. This list will reassure you that everything you are experiencing when woodburning for the first time is normal.

Handling the tool. Holding and burning with a woodburning tool will feel unfamiliar. Due to muscle memory, your fingers will want to hold and move the woodburning tool the same way you hold and write with a pen. Remember, you are transferring heat to a surface and not ink. You will need to train your brain with repetition and practice to hold and use your woodburning tool (especially if it is a thicker tool) so that it can do its job to burn wood. After some time, your tool will feel natural to hold and easy to burn with.

Slow process. Woodburning is a slow process. When I say slow, I mean like super slow. If it takes you three seconds to write your name with a pen on paper, it might take three minutes to burn it into wood. If you notice your wood is not getting dark when burning at a high heat setting, try burning at a slower speed. The hot nib must contact the wood long enough to transfer heat and create a burn mark. Keep in mind that some types of wood burn slower than others, and some tools operate at different temperatures even if they're on the same heat setting.

Applying pressure. You'll have to learn through practice the amount of pressure you have to apply when using a solid-nib woodburning tool. Solid-nib tools do not reach extremely high temperatures at their highest heat setting, so you will have to apply more pressure down into the wood to create dark burn marks, especially when burning dense hardwoods such as birch. A solid-nib tool can withstand more pressure than a wire-nib tool. When a wired nib is heated on a high-heat setting, it becomes malleable and bends under pressure. However, you can easily burn denser hardwoods at a high-heat setting using light pressure with wire-nib tools.

Wood types. You will notice that each wood product or canvas burns differently. Some woods will burn faster and easier than others. I suggest burning as many different types of wood as you can to discover your wood preference. The best wood for beginners to burn on is basswood. It is a hardwood but falls on the soft end of the density spectrum. It burns easily and is widely accessible and inexpensive.

Individual preferences. When starting out, it's natural to search for the tools, nibs, and techniques that experienced artists are using. You will soon find out that everyone has an individual preference. As you begin to practice woodburning, you will notice that a certain tool, nibs, and techniques work better for you. No tool or nib is the best in the woodburning world. It all comes down to choosing the tool, nibs, and techniques that are accessible to you and allow you to have a comfortable, relaxing, and creative woodburning experience.

What to Expect with Practice

Here are some things to expect after you've practiced woodburning for some time. After practicing woodburning for days, months, or years, you will notice yourself burning with more ease and fluidity than when you started. This list will inspire you as a beginner to keep practicing until you can check off a few or all of these experiences.

Woodburning feels familiar. Holding and using the tool begins to feel natural, like it is an extension of your being. There is less conscious thought about how you will burn a part of your design. Instead, you burn instinctively, the same way you write your name with a pen on paper. You don't think about how you're going to move the pen around to create the letters. You just write.

Burning faster. You complete projects faster than when you were a beginner. When you master your woodburning tool and techniques, inevitably, you burn projects faster. You execute woodburning techniques smoother and more efficiently, with less time spent correcting errors. You develop a flow when woodburning designs.

Stronger grip. As a beginner, you will notice that gripping the tool and burning can feel like a lot of physical work for your hand. As you practice woodburning, you are working out all the little muscles in your hand, wrist, and fingers. With consistency and repetition, those muscles become stronger and create muscle memory for woodburning. Your hands will adjust to the amount of pressure and grip strength required to burn designs for long periods.

Wood knowledge. After burning enough projects on different types of wood, you begin to develop a wood preference and gain wood knowledge. You may prefer the way one wood burns easier than another. You may prefer the look and color of one wood type over another. You also understand how to burn and adjust your techniques slightly when burning a softwood versus a hardwood.

Confidence. You gain confidence, trusting yourself and your abilities, even in the face of a challenge. When you master woodburning techniques, you feel confident in burning any style of design within your creative ability. You are also confident in yourself to continuously learn and achieve new skills by stepping out of your comfort zone and challenging yourself with harder woodburning designs.

About the Author

COURT O'REILLY is a Canadian woodburning artist, yoga instructor, and nature lover. She has completed more than 300 commissions, shipping her art worldwide. Her favorite pieces to work on are portraits, geometric designs, and anything related to the outdoors.

In addition, Court collaborates with local woodworkers to create custom charcuterie boards, wood signs, live-edge tables, live-edge coasters, and many other wood products.

If Court is not woodburning, you can find her painting nature scenes in watercolor and acrylic paint in her studio.

For more info, please visit www.hippienorth.com and @hippienorth. ❋

Getting Started

Choosing a Woodburning Tool

The solid-nib tool takes a few minutes to heat up and a few minutes to cool down. The highest temperature setting on a solid-nib tool does not get as hot as a wire-nib woodburning tool. It still gets hot enough to create dark burn marks, you will just have to burn a little slower and apply more pressure down into the wood. Select a solid-nib tool with a variable temperature setting, various nibs, and a rubber grip handle for a better woodburning experience.

> **PROs:** inexpensive, variety of nibs, portable, variable temperature settings
>
> **CONs:** thicker grip handle, takes a few minutes to heat up and cool down, does not reach extremely high temperatures to burn faster and darker

Solid-Nib Woodburning Tools

Solid-nib woodburning tools are the best option for beginners. They are inexpensive and have a variety of nib choices.

The grip on the solid-nib tool is much thicker than an ink pen and will require you to adjust to the thickness. The nibs are made of solid metal and perform well under large amounts of pressure when woodburning. The nibs are interchangeable and twist in and out of the tool using pliers. Sometimes the nibs become loose in the tool shaft, requiring you to twist them back in gently with needle-nose pliers to continue burning.

Wire-Nib Woodburning Tools

A wire-nib woodburning tool is the more expensive option but performs the best when woodburning. A lightweight cord connects the wire-nib tool to a small compact station where you can control the temperature setting and turn the machine off and on.

A wire-nib tool has a slender grip like an ink pen, which creates a more comfortable woodburning

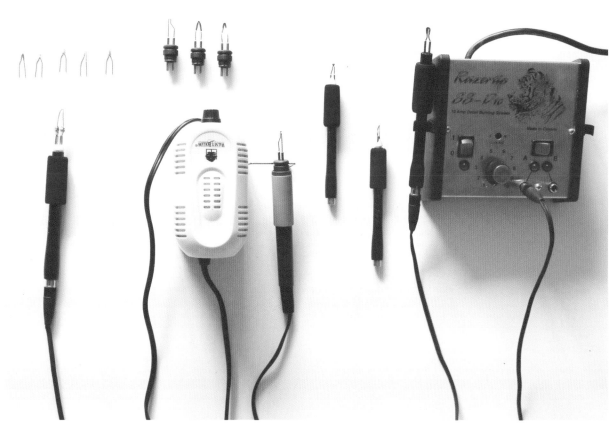

experience for your dominant hand. As the name suggests, the nibs are molded and shaped using a metal wire, and they are more delicate than solid nibs.

> **PROs:** slender grip feels similar to holding a pen, largest variety of nibs, higher temperature setting, burns faster, interchangeable nibs and pens, nibs heat up and cool down almost instantly
>
> **CONs:** expensive to purchase the woodburning system, expensive to replace fixed-tip pens, still portable, but temperature station unit may be heavy and bulky, some nibs are delicate and break easily without mindful burning practices

The wire nibs are either fixed to the woodburning pen (giving it the name fixed-tip pen), or they are interchangeable. If the wire nib is fixed to the pen and the nib breaks, you will have to replace the entire pen. If the nib is interchangeable, it is either fixed to a small base unit that quickly clicks in and out of the top of the pen, or the nib is one small piece of wire that screws into the top of the pen.

These nibs reach extremely high temperatures on the maximum heat setting, and they burn wood fast and with precision. However, the high temperatures can cause the nibs to become red hot and possibly bend or break under very little pressure. You will need to learn each nib's temperature and pressure threshold.

Using a Woodburning Tool

Prepare Your Workspace

Be sure to read and follow all of the manufacturer's safety instructions when using this tool. Before you turn your tool on, prepare your workspace for woodburning. Choose a place in your home that receives lots of light. Natural light is best, but a bright light or lamp is good, too. If possible, set up near an open window or use a fan to maximize ventilation when you burn wood. Give yourself plenty of tabletop space to reduce the possibility of materials touching a hot tool. Use a sturdy table or desk.

If applicable, use the metal holder that comes with your solid-nib tool kit to avoid burning the tabletop when your tool is on. Tape down the holder to keep the hot tool from sliding off and falling onto the floor. If your tool's cord is not long enough to reach an electrical outlet from your workstation, use an extension cord.

Temperature

Temperature dials on solid-nib tools and wire-nib tools have a range of low-, medium-, and high-heat settings using a color-coded system or numbers. There are also on and off settings to ensure you turn the heat completely off when the tool is not in use. Low heat at the yellow or lowest number heat setting will create a light brown burn mark. Medium heat at the orange or middle number heat setting will create a medium brown burn mark. High heat at the red or highest number range will create a dark brown or black burn mark.

Each brand and type of tool will vary in temperature compared to another, even at the same low, medium, and high heat settings. Some tools may burn a medium brown at their medium temperature setting, while others may burn dark brown at their medium temperature setting. If you are burning a specific color in your woodburning design, you will have to adjust the heat setting for your particular tool until you find the temperature that achieves light, medium, and dark brown burn colors.

temperature as you burn. The cord should fall to the inside of your dominant hand's arm. Your hand will also have to hold the wood steady as you burn.

Hold a wire-nib tool similarly to how you grip a pen. The cord that connects the pen to the compact temperature station is usually lightweight and does not interfere with woodburning. You do not need to hold the cord with your opposite hand.

Holding Your Tool

For solid-nib tools that have the temperature dial on the cord, I suggest holding the tool with your dominant hand and using your other hand to hold the cord gently. The weight of the dial can pull down on the cord, making the tool feel heavy in your dominant hand. By holding the cord in your other hand, you alleviate the pressure placed on the tool, and you have easy access to the dial to change the

Nibs

What Is a Nib?

A nib, by definition, is the pointed end part of a pen. When referring to a woodburning tool, the nib is the solid metal or wire piece at the end of the tool that gets hot and transfers heat to a surface. Interchangeable nibs twist, plug, or screw into the end of the woodburning tool's shaft. There are a variety of nibs available for every type of woodburning tool, and each one is designed for specific purposes.

Each nib is molded and shaped to perform one or two woodburning techniques really well. However, I try not to limit and categorize nibs to burning

specific details because it reduces creativity when woodburning. Nibs are extremely versatile, and many artists use different nibs to burn the same style of lines, dots, and shading. There is no wrong way a nib can be applied and burn.

When you think about it, every woodburning design is made up of straight lines, curved lines, dots, and shading. Therefore, try a bunch of different nibs and apply them to burning straight lines, curved lines, dots, and shading, and see which nibs you like the best!

Types of Nibs and Application

For straight lines. Use a nib with a long, sharp, thin, and straight edge, also known as a knife-edge nib.

For curved lines and dots. Use a nib with a ball stylus or a rounded or curved end. The nib should not contain any flat or sharp edges.

For shading. Use a nib with a large surface area that is either flat or round like a bowl. A nib with a large surface area can burn more space at a time, which speeds up the shading process.

For small details. Use the same nib you would use to burn straight lines, curved lines, dots, or shading, and apply the woodburning technique on a smaller scale to burn tiny details. You can also use a nib with a smaller or finer tip.

Removing and Changing Nibs

Always treat your nibs as if they are hot. This creates a good habit of removing your nibs using tools rather than your fingers. You might just forget to turn off your tool and accidentally handle the hot nib with your fingers! Before you remove your nib from your tool, let the nib cool down. Hot nibs are malleable and prone to warping, bending, and breaking when handled.

Solid-nib tools. Use a pair of needle-nose pliers to twist solid nibs in and out. If the nib is still warm once you remove it, place it in a small ceramic dish to avoid burning the tabletop. If the nib becomes loose while burning, you can gently use pliers to twist the hot nib back into the tool until you feel resistance. If you twist too hard and too tight, the nib can break off or strip the threading in the tool shaft, making it impossible to get the nib back out.

Wire-nib, fixed-tip pen. These nibs are fixed to the woodburning pen. You must change the entire pen by unplugging the cord at the bottom of the pen and connecting a new pen with a different nib.

Wire-nib tool with base unit. These nibs are fixed to a small base unit that clicks in and out of the top of the woodburning pen. Use metal tongs to remove the nib, and use your fingers to click in the new (not hot) nib.

Wire-nib tool with single wire. These nibs require a small screwdriver to loosen two screws connected to the top of the woodburning pen to release the small wire nib. Once the nib is loose, remove the nib and place a new nib onto the top of the pen. Twist the screws back in to secure the nib in place.

Nibs for This Book

I primarily used the universal solid nib and the rounded solid nib for this book because they are the most common and accessible nibs for beginners. These nibs are included in most solid-nib woodburning tool kits. If you do not have these two nibs, or you are using a wire-nib woodburning tool, then use the nibs you do have that are similar in nature to woodburn straight lines, curved lines, dots, and shading.

Universal solid nib. This nib is ideal for burning straight lines, curved lines, shading, and fine details, hence the name *universal*. It is composed of a sharp edge for burning lines and a flat edge for burning shading. For this book only, I will call the top of the sharp edge the *head* and the bottom of the sharp edge the *heel*. These two terms enhance the woodburning instructions in this book's technique and project sections. Hold the woodburning tool so that the longer edge, the *head,* is at the top and the shorter edge, the *heel*, is at the bottom.

Rounded solid nib. This nib is ideal for burning dots and curved lines. It has a rounded end that resembles a sphere, making it perfect for burning circular dots and flowing along curves.

Cleaning Nibs

Care and maintenance of your nibs are important to preserve their lifespan and create an overall better woodburning experience. You will notice when you are woodburning that a black residue of carbon builds up on the end of the nib. It is wood matter that has burned and solidified on your nib due to constant pressure and heat. It acts as a barrier between your hot nib and the wood, preventing heat from being transferred. Therefore, immediate attention is required to clean off the carbon so you can continue woodburning.

Strop and white compound (aluminum oxide). This technique is recommended for all nib styles for both solid nibs and wire nibs when the nib is cooled

down. This is ultimately the best cleaning practice for your nibs. It causes zero wear and tear on your nibs, removes carbon with ease, and even polishes your nibs to have a sparkling finish. You can use powdered aluminum oxide or a solid bar of aluminum oxide.

To clean your nibs using this technique, let your nib cool down. Load the rough side of the leather strop with your chosen aluminum oxide. Rub your cooled nib in the aluminum oxide until the carbon falls off. The grit from the aluminum oxide will remove buildup with ease. Flip the strop over and rub your nib on the smooth side for a sparkly polished finish. If you do not have aluminum oxide, you can use the rough side of the leather strop while your tool is still hot to get most of the carbon buildup off.

Brass metal brush. This technique is recommended for all solid and wire nib styles, but use an extra-gentle hand with wire nibs. This method is used to remove carbon on the nib when the nib is still hot for a quick clean while woodburning. Use only a brush with soft bristles to avoid scratching your nibs. Solid nibs can handle more aggressive cleaning methods without experiencing much wear and tear. However, thin and delicate wire nibs can scratch easily if you are not gentle. If a wire nib with a thin straight edge or flat surface gets a hairline scratch, it will be noticeable in the burn mark it creates.

To clean your nibs using this technique, scrape the carbon buildup off a hot or cool nib gently with the metal brush. Remember that when a metal nib is hot, it is more malleable and prone to scratches.

Sandpaper. This technique is recommended for all solid nib styles. It is not recommended for wire nibs. Sandpaper is usually the most accessible cleaning material, but it is also the most damaging to your nibs over time. Sandpaper will scrape off the carbon buildup, but it will also scrape and wear down the metal of the nibs. If you choose sandpaper for a quick clean here and there, use extra-fine grit sandpaper only, like 320-grit or higher. Sandpaper can take off most of the carbon buildup and be used while the nib is hot or cold. If your wire nib needs a quick clean and you only have access to sandpaper, use this cleaning method with extra care and gentleness when the nib has cooled down.

To clean your nibs using this technique, lightly and quickly rub carbon off a solid nib while it is hot or cold. You can use a sheet or a block of extra-fine grit sandpaper. If the nib is hot, make sure your fingers aren't directly opposite it on the other side of the sandpaper in case the nib burns a hole through the sheet.

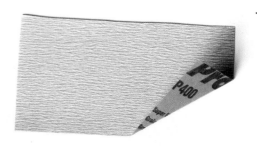

Wood

Selecting Wood

There is an overwhelming selection of wood canvases and wooden items made using a variety of wood species. You want to choose a safe and suitable wood to burn for your project. It's a good idea to become a bit of a wood expert so you know exactly what to look for when you are sourcing and purchasing wood.

Softwood versus hardwood. Softwood comes from coniferous trees, also known as evergreen trees, such as pine and cedar. Softwoods are less dense and less heat resistant. They burn easily at lower temperatures, and their wood structure is softer and less durable. Their density ranges from soft varieties like pine to harder varieties like cedar.

Hardwood comes from deciduous trees that lose their leaves annually, such as maple and birch. Hardwoods are denser and more heat resistant. They require hotter temperatures to achieve dark burn marks, and their wood structure is harder and more durable. Their density ranges from soft varieties like basswood to harder varieties like ash.

Wood grain. Wood grain is the alternating dark and light regions in a piece of wood that create unique color patterns on the wood surface. Wood grain can be greatly spaced out or tightly packed together. Woods with an even grain color, such as birch and basswood, display an evenly distributed color across the wood surface. Woods with a strong grain color, such as pine and oak, display a range of prominent alternating light and dark regions.

Wood grain can add character to your woodburning, but it can also interfere with detailed art. The darker and lighter regions of the grain can also burn at different temperatures. For example, the dark fibrous rings in pine burn like a hard hardwood, while the white regions burn like a soft softwood.

Safe wood. The safest wood to burn is unfinished raw wood. Select wood that has absolutely no wood seal or finish because it is toxic to burn and hazardous to your health. A wood finish adds a matte or gloss appearance to the surface and darkens the wood grain color. If you are not sure if there is a finish on your wood, do not burn it.

Avoid woodburning on pressure-treated wood and MDF because these contain toxic chemicals. Reclaimed barn wood and driftwood can be toxic because it is hard to determine their wood type and if there is a wood finish present from their previous lives.

Wood collected outside from a fallen or cut tree is safe to burn only when dry. The wood should be kiln-dried or air-dried to a moisture meter reading of 6% before you burn it.

Burning green wood (wood with a high moisture content) from outside can release mold or other toxic organic material.

Be extra cautious with plywood. Plywood is composed of thin layers of engineered sheets of wood bound together using an adhesive. This adhesive can be toxic to burn if you burn deep enough through the wood layer into the glue layer.

Common Woods for Woodburning

Now that you have some wood knowledge under your belt, it's time to discuss the best woods to work with for woodburning. This really comes down to individual preference, accessibility, and cost. To develop a preference for wood, you will have to burn as many types of wood species and products to determine your favorites.

Most artists, including me, prefer soft hardwoods with a light grain color and a smooth, sanded surface because you can burn them with precision at all temperature settings across their uniform grain color. My go-to woods for burning are basswood, cherry, aspen, alder, linden, soft maple, and poplar wood. Their grain colors range from light brown to light red. They are receptive to every type of nib and woodburning technique. In addition, I also love working with hard hardwoods such as birch, hard maple, and ash.

The most commonly selected wood for woodburning is basswood, a soft hardwood with light color and even grain.

When choosing wood for any woodburning project, you can select a softwood or hardwood and your preferred grain style. What's most important is that the wood is dry, raw (no seal or finish), smooth, and safe. Whether it is a wooden box, spoon, slab, sign, coaster, or any other wooden item, it must possess those important qualities for woodburning.

Where to Purchase Wood

Craft stores, online markets, and lumber stock shops all carry unfinished raw wood products and slabs ready for safe woodburning. Craft stores usually carry inexpensive wood options with a light-colored grain such as pine, cedar, basswood, and birch.

Lumber stock shops are a great option to find a unique selection of kiln-dried or air-dried wood with varying grain colors. They tend to carry a wide selection of hardwoods in many sizes and styles that you wouldn't normally find at your local craft store. These items can be more expensive than what you'd purchase at a craft store, and some slabs may require you to plane and sand the wood to create a smooth surface for burning.

Preparing Wood

Preparing your wood by sanding the surface with ultra-fine grit sandpaper is an essential step to woodburning with ease and accuracy. A super-smooth wood surface is the most receptive to heat and will allow you to woodburn faster than if your wood has a rough surface.

Some wood products are pre-sanded, like most wooden items found in craft stores. If you run your finger over the surface of the wood, it should feel like you are touching glass. If it feels coarse, rough, or fuzzy, I suggest sanding the surface by hand or using a random orbital electric hand sander with 320-grit sandpaper or higher. After sanding, wipe the wood surface with a dry, clean cloth to remove dust.

Wood Finishes

Choosing a Finish

Applying a wood finish after burning helps preserve the integrity of the wood and the woodburning artwork. There are different wood finishes to choose from depending on the function of your wooden item, your preferred look of the wood grain color, the amount of time you have (cure times vary between minutes and days), and cost.

For food boards and utensils. Use a food-grade wood finish. These are non-toxic finishes that are safe to place food directly on. Food-grade finishes include mineral oil, pure tung oil, raw linseed oil, and beeswax.

For coasters. Use a heat-resistant, water-resistant wood finish. Danish oil is the best choice. When it cures, it has a matte finish that provides heat and water resistance for those hot cups of coffee and condensation from cold drinks.

For wall art and signs. Use any clear water-based wood finish, or leave the project natural. Wall art and signs receive minimal wear and tear, which means they do not need a highly durable wood finish or any finish at all. A clear finish such as polycrylic or water-based polyurethane is a great choice to preserve the high contrast of the woodburning art and keep the wood grain light in color.

For painted art. If your artwork contains watercolor or acrylic paint, use a clear spray-on wood finish to avoid spreading the paint. You can keep the wood raw as long as you keep it inside away from direct sunlight to prevent the wood and artwork from fading.

Raw wood with natural grain color

Clear polycrylic, clear water-based polyurethane, or water-based spar urethane

Danish oil or oil-based spar urethane

Mineral oil or butcher block oil

Tung oil

Dark stain

For outdoor items. Use an oil-based or water-based spar urethane. This wood finish is completely waterproof when cured and protects against nature's toughest elements, including UV damage. The oil-based option will add a warm color to your wood grain, while the water-based option cures with a crystal-clear finish.

For multipurpose items. Use any wood finish of your choice. A wood item, such as a tray or box, will require a wood finish to protect the wood from scratches, dents, and wear and tear. All wood finishes provide protection, so it is up to you if you want a clear finish or to add a stain color. Avoid using a stain color that is too dark to keep your woodburning art from disappearing in the dark wood grain.

Finish Examples

At the left are basswood slices with a variety of finishes applied. Each type of wood you use will darken at different strengths, hues, and tones after applying a finish. For example, cherry wood results in a warm red grain color when Danish oil is applied. The colors you see here are specific to basswood.

All wood finishes will cause the wood grain color to appear much darker when first applied. Wait until the finish is dry and cured to see the true color of the wood grain. Always test your finish of choice on a piece of scrap wood if you are unsure what the cured appearance of the finish will look like before you apply it to your artwork. Dark stain is not recommended for woodburning art because the art will be difficult to see on the wood.

Always read the manufacturer's label for each finish for safe application practices and clean-up instructions.

Other Materials

Graphite paper. This is the key material for transferring a pattern onto wood. The dark black side of graphite paper contains graphite or carbon that transfers onto the wood when you trace a pattern  on top of it with a pen or pencil. One sheet of graphite paper can be used multiple times until the graphite stops transferring.

Metal ruler. A handy tool for burning straight lines by gently pressing the hot nib against the ruler to guide your line.

Hooks. These are not essential, but they're a great way to hang woodburning art on a wall!

Paint. You can use watercolor or acrylic paints to add some color to any art piece after burning. Paint directly onto the wood!

Micro-jet torch. This tool makes it easy to burn large dark or black areas. Find a torch with adjustable airflow to adjust the size of the flame for more accurate burning. Be sure to read and follow all of the manufacturer's safety instructions when using this tool.

Tools Checklist

Here are all the tools and materials you'll need to complete the projects in this book!

ESSENTIALS

- Solid-nib woodburning tool with variable temperature settings (you can still follow along with a wire-nib tool!)
- Universal solid nib (or a nib with a straight sharp edge for lines and a large surface nib for shading)
- Rounded solid nib (or a nib with a ball stylus or rounded end)
- Needle-nose pliers (or a tool capable of removing your nibs from your tool safely)
- Wood
- Graphite paper
- Pen or pencil
- Tape
- Scissors
- Access to printer
- Safety equipment such as a fan, mask, or gloves

NONESSENTIALS (. . . but handy!)

- Sandpaper or random orbit electric hand sander
- Nib cleaning materials
- Metal ruler
- Watercolor and/or acrylic paint with brushes
- Wood finish and application materials
- Hooks and/or twine with corresponding installation tools
- Non-slip mat
- Micro-jet torch
- Erasing tool like a utility knife

Safety

Here are a few safety considerations to help keep your woodburning hobby safe, healthy, and efficient!

Tool Safety

All metal exposed on the tool and nib is hot when the tool is on.

If your tool falls off the table, do not try to catch it. You may accidentally grab the hot metal part. Let the tool fall on the ground before picking it up safely.

Do not change nibs using your fingers. Turn off the tool before each nib change and allow the nib to cool down. Use pliers or metal tongs to twist or pull each nib in and out. If a solid nib loosens while burning, use pliers to gently twist it back into the tool shaft.

Tape a metal hook to your tabletop to safely rest your solid-nib tool in. Always rest your hot tool in a docking station when you need to put it down.

Always turn the tool off when not in use. Do not leave a hot tool unattended. Unplug your tool when you are finished.

Read the safety guidelines from the tool's manufacturer.

Wood

Do not use wood that is sealed or chemically treated. Never burn pressure-treated wood or MDF.

Use dry wood. Burning green wood (wood with moisture) can release pockets of moisture that may contain toxic residue or mold. This applies to wood from a freshly fallen or cut tree.

Use wood that is dry, raw (no wood finish), smooth, and safe.

Burning

Use sufficient ventilation when burning. Burn near an open window, use a fan to blow smoke away from your face, or wear a mesh mask with an active carbon filter. These options will help protect your lungs and eyes.

Do not burn with your face directly over the wood to avoid inhaling smoke.

Use a flexible and comfortable leather glove to hold the tool while woodburning if you feel the handle is too hot.

Make sure your workspace is clean and materials are spaced far enough apart so they do not overlap and touch the hot tool.

Work at a sturdy desk or table.

Wood Finish

Always read the manufacturer's label and guidelines for application, safety, and cleanup.

10 Fundamental Woodburning Techniques

THESE TEN TECHNIQUES are the foundation that a woodburning hobby is built on. By learning them, you will be able to complete any woodburning project from start to finish with ease and confidence. Once you've mastered these techniques, you can apply them to the projects in the second half of this book to advance your creativity and woodburning skills.

I am demonstrating these techniques with the two most common and versatile nibs found in most beginner and intermediate solid-nib woodburning toolkits—the universal solid nib and the rounded solid nib. If you do not have this tool or nibs, I recommend following along with the tool and nibs you do have that closely match. For line work, use a nib with a straight sharp edge. For shading, use a nib with a flat surface area. For dots and curved lines, use a nib with a rounded end.

There are a million and one ways to use each nib and burn creatively. I will teach you the methods I use personally. Feel free to burn and practice using different techniques and nibs outside of the ones I demonstrate with here. Every woodburning artist has an individual preference for nibs when burning lines, dots, and shading. Choose the techniques and nibs that feel the most natural to you and allow you to create a style of woodburning art that resonates with you.

Create a practice board to follow along and learn these ten techniques. An ideal practice board is a piece of scrap wood or a blank wood panel that is smooth, flat, and light-colored. If the wood feels rough to the touch, sand it using an electric hand sander or by hand with 320-grit sandpaper. Use the entire space on your practice board to learn and burn techniques. You can sand down the burn marks with an electric sander once the board is full and use it again. ❁

Creating a Pattern

The first step of a woodburning project is deciding what you would like to woodburn. If this is your first woodburning project, I suggest starting with a simple design with minimal detail, like a silhouette image or an outline of an image. Once you choose a woodburning design, find a piece of wood in your desired size and shape. Now you are ready to create a pattern!

STEP 1: Choose an Image

Draw your own image or search online. Use keywords like silhouette, outline, and simple when searching for an image to guarantee a beginner-level design. For example, anchor silhouette image or anchor outline pattern. Be mindful of copyright. If you are using an online image for profit, **use an image free of copyright**. Give credit to the artist where due.

STEP 2: Edit to Black and White

Woodburning is a monochrome art, meaning it uses only one color in various tones. Creating a pattern in black and white gives you a visual reference of where lighter and darker shading will be burned in your artwork. The various gray tones in the pattern directly reference light, medium, and dark shading in the woodburning.

If the pattern you have chosen has color, you will need to edit the image to black and white. You can do this on your computer by opening the color image in a photo program and decreasing the saturation value of the image to zero. This can also be done on your phone using a photo editing app. If you don't have access to an editing program or app, you can skip to the next step and print your color image in black and white.

Step 1

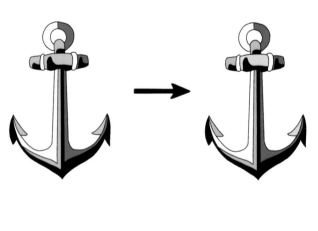

Step 2

STEP 3: Print

Print the pattern to fit on the piece of wood you would like to burn. It may take a few tries to get the printed image the exact size you want. I place my desired wood canvas on a blank piece of printer paper and visualize how large I need the printed image to be. A coaster may require a pattern printed on one-quarter of a piece of paper, while a large wood canvas may require the pattern to be printed across two or more sheets of paper.

I adjust the size of my pattern in a word processing document. For patterns requiring two or more sheets of paper, I expand the image larger than the document page. Then I copy and paste the image onto a second page so I have two identical images, both larger than their pages. I adjust the placement of the images on their respective pages so each page shows one-half of the total pattern. Then I print out the pages, align the images, and tape the pages together. Remember to adjust your printer setting to print in black and white if you could not edit the color image in the previous step.

Step 3

STEP 4: Cut Out the Pattern

Cut an even border around the entire printed pattern, leaving a small space between the cutting edge and the pattern outline. An evenly cut border around the pattern will help you place the pattern exactly in the position you want on your wood. If your printed pattern is on two or more sheets of paper, you will need to tape these pages together so each section of the pattern accurately lines up to create one large image.

Step 4

Transferring a Pattern

Transferring a pattern onto a piece of wood is the key to woodburning with precision and confidence! This step eliminates the need for any artistic experience because you can trace the pattern onto the wood and burn along the traced lines. Whether you are a beginner or an experienced woodburning artist, transferring a pattern is a common step in many woodburning projects.

STEP 1: Tape

Use scotch, masking, or painter's tape to secure your printed pattern to the wood. Tape down one side of the pattern only so you can lift the entire pattern off the wood as if you were turning a page in a book. Make sure the pattern cannot wiggle around.

STEP 2: Add Graphite Paper

Cut a piece of graphite paper to a size that matches your pattern. Slide the paper under the pattern. The dark black graphite side faces the wood, and the light gray side faces the pattern. The graphite is the substance that transfers onto the wood with the pressure from tracing. One sheet of graphite paper can be used repeatedly until it stops transferring onto the wood.

STEP 3: Trace

Use a fine-tip pen or pencil to trace your pattern. Apply the same amount of pressure as you would normally use to write. Trace every line in the pattern, occasionally lifting the pattern and graphite paper to check that each line is transferred onto the wood. Use a colored pen instead of black for tracing detailed patterns with many lines. This helps you see what you have traced so you don't miss any lines.

Be mindful of the weight of your tracing hand on the graphite paper. The weight of your wrist and hand can transfer graphite smudges onto the wood.

If an area in your design requires shading, you do not need to transfer this onto the wood. Leave the areas that require light, medium, and dark shading blank and refer to the pattern while burning to locate where you need to add each shade. For dark shading only, you can use my time-saving trick in the next step!

STEP 4: Mark Dark Shading

Here's a time-saving trick for marking areas that require dark shading. Instead of coloring in the areas completely when transferring the pattern, mark them with small X's. Only use this method for areas requiring dark shading because the marked X's will be burned over completely and disappear. If used to mark light and medium shading, the X's may still be visible after burning and interfere with the finished artwork.

Step 1

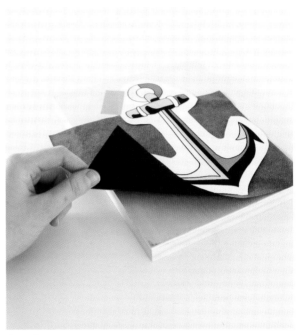

Step 2

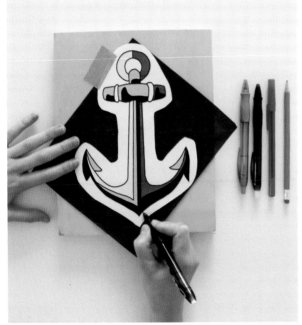

Step 3

Step 4

Burning Lines: Universal Solid Nib

When burning lines on wood, the universal solid nib or any sharp-edge nib acts like a hot knife in butter. It cuts through the wood grain to create a clean, uniform line. Burning lines with this nib feels different from drawing lines with a pencil. It requires more movement from your hand, wrist, and arm because the nib doesn't flow over the surface of the wood but instead carves into it. You may notice as you burn curved lines, you will have to rotate your wood to keep the direction of the line in front of you.

On your practice board, use a pencil to draw a few straight lines, curvy lines, and small shapes to practice burning with the universal solid nib.

Terminology

To guide you through this technique, for this book only, I will call the top point of the nib the *head* and the bottom point of the nib the *heel*. There is also a head and heel for most wire nibs with a sharp knife edge.

The Push-Away Method

STEP 1: Place the heel. Place the heel of the hot nib onto the wood at the end of the line closest to you. Lift the head of the nib above the wood surface slightly, pointing it in the direction of the line, away from you.

STEP 2: Burn the line. Apply pressure down onto the heel of the nib and begin to push the nib away from you along the traced line. Keep the pressure consistent and the head of the nib lifted above the wood surface slightly like the front of a boat moving through water.

The faster you move the nib and the less pressure you apply, the thinner your line will be. The slower you move the nib and the more pressure you apply, the thicker your line will be. You can make additional passes to get the line as dark and thick as desired. Adjust the tool's temperature to change the burn color: low heat for light lines, medium temperature for medium lines, and high heat for dark lines.

For curved lines, you can burn the entire line in one motion or burn in segments by stopping and starting to rotate the wood as you work.

The Pull-Toward Method

STEP 1: Place the head. Place the head of the hot nib onto the wood at the end of the line farthest from you. Lift the heel of the nib above the wood surface slightly, pointing it in the direction of the line toward you.

STEP 2: Burn the line. Apply pressure down onto the head of the nib and begin to pull the nib toward you along the traced line. Keep the pressure consistent and the heel of the nib lifted above the wood surface slightly like the front of a boat moving through water.

The Push-Away Method: Step 1

The Push-Away Method: Step 2

The Pull-Toward Method: Step 1

The Pull-Toward Method: Step 2

Burning Lines: Rounded Solid Nib

The rounded solid nib or any nib with a rounded end or ball stylus is a popular choice for burning dots, curves, and cursive writing. Many woodburners find burning with this nib similar to writing with a pen because of how the nib flows over the surface of the wood.

This nib requires an extra-steady hand to burn clean and uniform lines. It is a pressure-sensitive nib, meaning slight changes in pressure when burning will create thicker and thinner line sections. Sometimes the line can have a dotted look because the nib gets caught in the wood grain every inch or two, causing the nib to sink into the wood and burn dots. To avoid the dotted line, you can burn using the airplane technique described here.

On your practice board, use a pencil to draw a few straight lines, curvy lines, and small shapes to practice burning with the rounded solid nib.

STEP 1: Starting Motion

Before the hot nib touches the wood at the beginning of the line, the tool should be in motion, moving in the direction in which you will be burning the line. Visualize the nib as an airplane descending for landing. This movement will prevent you from creating a dot at the beginning of the line.

STEP 2: Burn the Line

As the nib touches the wood and begins to burn the line, keep the tool in constant motion until you need to lift the nib off the wood. Visualize the nib as an airplane landing and driving along the tarmac without slowing down. Keep the pressure consistent to avoid burning a dotted line.

The faster you move the nib and the less pressure you apply, the thinner your line will be. The slower you move the nib and the more pressure you apply, the thicker your line will be. You can make additional passes to get the line as dark and thick as desired. Adjust the temperature of the tool to change the burn color.

When using this nib, burn as much of the line as is comfortable for your hand and wrist in one motion before lifting the nib off. This applies to both straight and curved lines. The less you lift and move your hand when using this nib, the more uniform your line will be.

STEP 3: Finishing Motion

Keep the tool in motion when you lift the nib off the wood. Visualize the nib as an airplane driving down the tarmac and taking off. This movement will prevent you from creating a dot at the end of the line. Repeat Steps 1–3 as many times as necessary to burn the full length of the line.

STEP 4: Touchups

Burn over any dots created when burning the line. Go over the line, making it as thick as the dots, to give it a uniform thickness. Follow Steps 1–3 to burn the line from dot to dot.

Step 1

Step 2

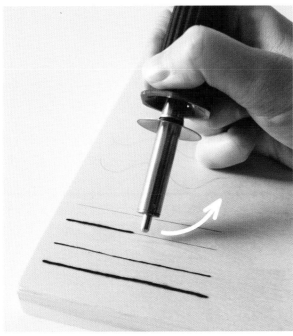

Step 3

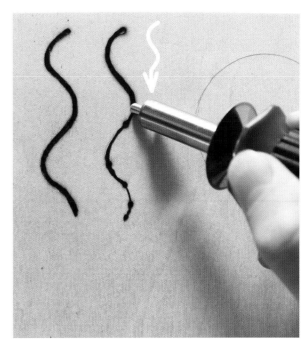

Step 4

Burning Solid Shading: Universal Solid Nib

The universal solid nib or any nib with a large flat surface area is a great option for burning solid uniform shading. The entire flat side of the universal solid nib is the area used for shading. Burning solid shading works the best on wood that is smooth and flat. The smoother the wood surface, the easier it is for the nib to glide and burn the shading accurately.

Different wood types will burn different shading hues, even if using the same temperature. Some woods will burn black shading at a high heat setting, while other woods may burn dark brown at the same heat setting. Adjust your nib temperature until you achieve and burn your preferred shading color. Make sure your wood is smooth and sanded using 320-grit sandpaper or higher for best results.

STEP 1: Position the Nib

The universal solid nib has a flat edge on each side of the sharp edge. You can identify these sections by their unique shape, which looks like half of an oval. The flat edge is what you use to burn shading—its large size speeds up the shading process. If you are right-handed, use the right flat edge by tilting your tool to the right at a 45-degree angle until the flat edge of the nib is flush with the wood surface. You may need to place your fingers higher up on the tool toward the cord to create a steep enough angle to get the nib flat on the wood. If you are left-handed, use the left flat edge of the tool by tilting the tool to the left at a 45-degree angle.

Practice burning with the flat edge of the nib on high heat until you can create the entire half-oval shape by pressing the nib down on the wood like a stamp. Once you can burn this shape, the angle at which you are holding the tool and the pressure you are applying are correct.

STEP 2: Practice the Movement

After mastering the nib placement on the wood, you are ready to add movement to burn shading. If you are right-handed, position the right flat edge of the nib on the wood and pull it to the right while keeping the tool at a 45-degree angle. If you are left-handed, use the left flat edge of the nib and pull it to the left.

Your fingers play an important role in creating shading by gripping the tool to keep the nib steady while also using strength to apply steady pressure. Burn slowly so the nib has time to create a dark burn mark on the wood.

STEP 3: Burn the Outline

When you need to shade an area in your woodburning design, I suggest burning a clean shaded border around the inner edge of the section first. This will speed up the process in the next step. With a thick border, you won't have to worry about going outside the lines when applying shading to the rest of the section.

Draw a few small shapes on your practice board. Glide the hot nib along the inside perimeter of each shape to create a thick shaded border. Move the wood around as you burn so you always have a comfortable hand placement. For small areas that require shading but can't fit the entire flat edge of the universal nib, lift the heel of the nib off the wood slightly to use the top portion of the flat edge to burn the shading.

STEP 4: Fill in the Shape

Fill in the remaining area to be shaded by burning thick marks with the flat edge of the nib. You can create thick horizontal marks, one on top of the other, or burn as if you are scribbling with a marker, using slow up and down movements as you pull the nib either left or right. Burn over the shading if necessary until it is uniform and very dark.

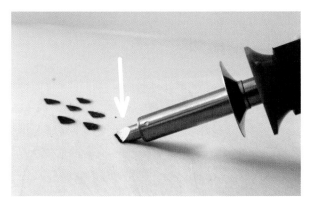

Step 1

Step 2

Step 3

Step 4

Burning Other Shading Patterns: Universal Solid Nib

You can use several techniques with the universal solid nib to create different tones and textures of shading. Shading's finished appearance depends on the nib's temperature while burning. A low temperature setting results in light shading, a medium temperature setting results in medium shading, and a high temperature setting results in dark shading. You can also use speed and pressure to vary the color of shading. For example, you can use the high heat setting and achieve light shading by burning quickly and with light pressure.

Draw a grid of squares on your practice board. Then practice burning each shading pattern in light, medium, dark, and a gradient. Remember that different wood types will produce different shading colors.

PATTERN 1: Solid Fill Shading

Use the flat edge of the universal nib to burn solid shading to fill in a square. Use low heat for light shading, medium heat for medium shading, and high heat for dark shading. Take your time to create a uniform color.

Then try your hand at gradient shading. You can create a gradient by working in sections, adjusting the heat setting on your tool to vary the shading color. Or, to create the shading with one continuous movement, you can use pressure to vary the shading color.

Start at one side of the square and apply heavy pressure to create dark shading. As you glide your nib to the left or right, begin to reduce the pressure on the nib to create medium shading. Use the

Pattern 1

Pattern 2

lightest pressure on the opposite side of the square to create light shading.

PATTERN 2: Thick Lines

Use the sharp edge of the universal solid nib to burn thick parallel lines. Burn slowly and use heavy pressure, placing the lines close together with little space between them. Use low heat for light shading, medium heat for medium shading, and high heat for dark shading. Then try a gradient version, varying the heat or pressure to transition the color from dark to light across the square.

PATTERN 3: Crisscross Lines

Use the sharp edge of the universal solid nib and normal pressure to burn a crisscross pattern of thin vertical and horizontal lines. The further apart you position the lines, the lighter the shading will appear. The closer you position the lines, the darker the shading will appear. Use low heat and position the lines far apart for light shading. Use medium heat and position the lines closer together for medium shading. Use high heat and position the lines very close together for dark shading. Then try a gradient version, varying the heat or pressure and line spacing to transition the color from dark to light across the square.

PATTERN 4: Thin Lines

Use the sharp edge of the universal solid nib on high heat to burn thin dark lines. Use light pressure and a fast burning speed. Position the lines far apart for light shading, closer together for medium shading, and very close for dark shading. Then try a gradient version, varying the line spacing to transition the color from dark to light across the square.

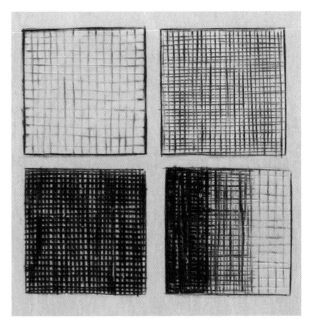

Pattern 3

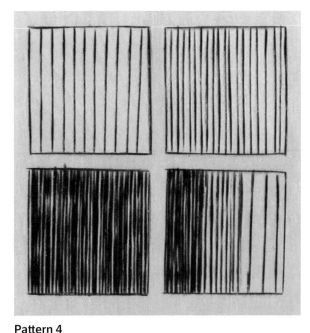

Pattern 4

Burning Dot Shading: Rounded Solid Nib

Dot shading, or stippling, is a time-consuming and repetitive process that yields beautiful results. Burning dots for shading creates a unique dimpled texture in the wood. Once you learn how to burn one dot, you can burn a million dots. It's super easy! You can burn large dots, small dots, dots in uniform rows, dots at random, dots in chevron patterns, or dots in a circular pattern to fill in any space on your woodburning design. It is a fun way to be creative with your woodburning art.

STEP 1: Practice Individual Dots

With the tool on high heat, press the nib down into the wood using heavy pressure. You can hold the tool straight up and down so the very tip of the nib burns the dot, or you can hold the tool like a pencil so the top side of the nib burns the dot. Press the nib into the wood for one to two seconds to burn a large dot. Press the nib into the wood for a quick half-second to burn a small dot. The larger the dots, the more textured the shading will appear.

Use your practice board to practice burning individual dots. Practice burning both large and small dots to get comfortable with the amount of pressure and time you need to use for each one.

STEP 2: Burn the Outline

Burn dots along the outline of an area that requires dot shading. Place the dots next to each other, burning directly on top of the pattern line to cover it. Use the space on your practice board to burn the outline of a circle.

STEP 3: Fill with Uniform Dot Shading

Fill in the circle with uniform rows of dots of the same size. Place the dots and the rows close together with no space between them.

STEP 4: Fill with Random Dot Shading

Repeat Step 2 to burn the outline of another circle. Fill in the circle randomly with dots of different sizes placed with no pattern. Place the dots close together with no space between them.

Step 1

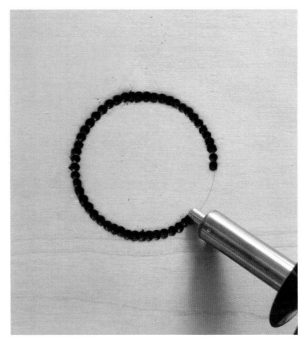

Step 2

Step 3

Step 4

Burning Other Shading Patterns: Rounded Solid Nib

The rounded solid nib or any nib with a rounded end burns shading with unique textures and patterns. Shading's finished appearance depends on the nib's temperature while burning. A low temperature setting results in light shading, a medium temperature setting results in medium shading, and a high temperature setting results in dark shading. You can also use speed and pressure to vary the color of shading.

Draw a grid of squares on your practice board. Then practice burning each shading pattern in light, medium, dark, and a gradient. Remember that different wood types will produce different shading colors.

PATTERN 1: Large Dots

Use the rounded solid nib with heavy pressure to burn large dots to fill in a square. Place the dots very close together in a uniform or random pattern. This creates a dimpled texture on the wood. Use low heat for light shading, medium heat for medium shading, and high heat for dark shading. Then try a gradient version, varying the heat to transition the color from dark to light across the square.

PATTERN 2: Lines

Use the rounded solid nib with heavy pressure to burn thick parallel lines, creating a striped texture. Place the lines close together with little space between them. Use low heat for light shading, medium heat for medium shading, and high heat for dark shading. Then try a gradient version, varying the heat to transition the color from dark to light across the square.

PATTERN 3: Swirls

Use the rounded solid nib to burn thin and thick lines in a random looping, swirling pattern. Use varying pressure and overlap the swirls to fill the space. Use low heat for light shading, medium heat for medium shading, and high heat for dark shading. Then try a gradient version, varying the heat to transition the color from dark to light across the square. Because you are using varying pressure, there will also be some variation in the burn color, creating an abstract look.

PATTERN 4: Small Dots

Use the universal rounded nib on high heat and light pressure to burn small dark dots. Position the dots far apart for light shading, closer together for medium shading, and very close for dark shading. Then try a gradient version, varying the spacing of the dots to transition the color from dark to light across the square.

Pattern 1

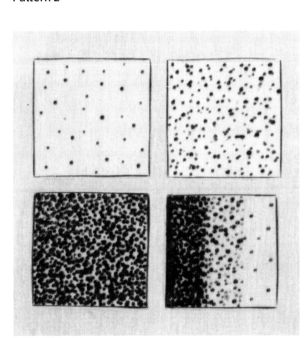

Pattern 2

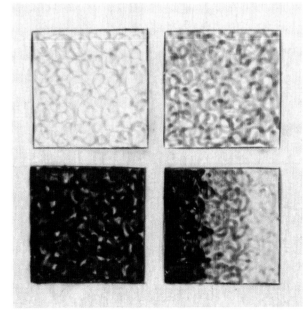

Pattern 3

Pattern 4

Burning Fur or Feather Detail: Universal Solid Nib

Woodburning fur detail is similar to woodburning hair detail in portraits or grass detail in landscape artwork. I use the universal solid nib for woodburning all types of fur of different lengths, styles, and colors in my artwork. Before practicing this technique, take some time to study a few black and white images of animals with fur to understand the flow and placement of the strands on different parts of the animal's body. The technique and temperature setting you use will depend on the type of fur you want to reproduce.

STEP 1: Practice

Use the sharp edge of the universal solid nib to burn wispy lines for fur detail. One line equals one fur strand. Use the push or pull technique (page 38) to create each line. Place the fur strands so they are staggered randomly. Some strands should angle slightly left and right, and each strand should slightly vary in length, thickness, and curvature to enhance the realistic look of the fur (1a). Avoid burning rows of straight lines stacked on top of one another because this appears uniform and unrealistic (1b).

Fur strands can be short, long, thin, thick, straight, wavy, light, or dark, depending on the type of fur you are woodburning. Adjust the tool's temperature to burn light, medium, and dark fur.

Use your practice board to try your hand at burning fur. Try using high heat to burn dark wispy strands at random.

STEP 2: Start Burning at the Top

When burning fur in a design, start at the top of the fur section and work your way down. Burn fur strands of your desired length and color in a random staggered formation. The strands can overlap one another slightly. The closer the strands are together, the more full the fur will appear.

Draw a square on your practice board. Use the tool on high heat to fill the top with dark wispy fur strands on high heat. Pack the strands closely together with a bit of space between them.

STEP 3: Match the Fur's Direction

Fur strands change direction on different parts of an animal. Be sure to account for this when burning fur in your design, making sure your strands flow in a natural direction. Use black and white reference photos of the animal you are burning to see how the fur flows over its body. Use the same technique as in Step 2 to burn the fur strands, and simply change the direction of your strokes to account for the flow of the fur. Practice curving the direction of the fur strands to the left or right in the square on your practice board.

STEP 4: Add Shading

Use the flat edge of the universal nib to add shading on top of the fur. Be sure the shading color is lighter than the color of the fur strands so that the fur texture can be seen through the shading. When adding shading, move the tool to follow the flow and direction of the fur. Use medium heat to add medium shading to the square on your practice board.

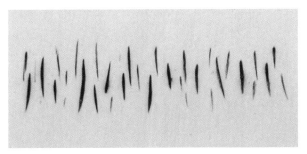

Step 1a

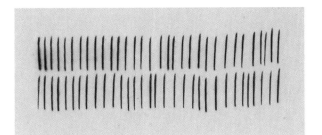

Step 1b

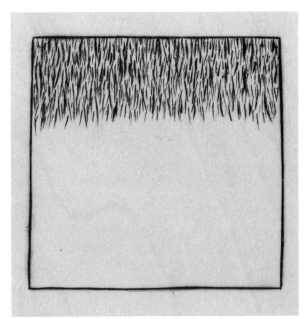

Step 2

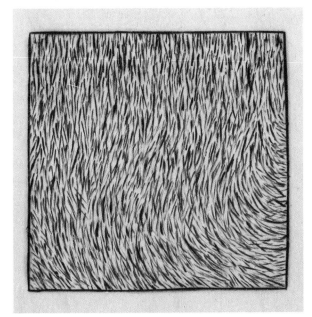

Step 3

Step 4

Erasing Errors

Learning any new craft requires practice and lots of trial and error. Not every project will come out perfectly, and that's okay! Here are some methods to remove stray burn and graphite marks from your designs. Use these to touch up your finished art.

Rubber or Sand Eraser

These are both good options for removing unwanted graphite marks on the wood. Start with a rubber eraser, vigorously rubbing the graphite mark until it disappears. If the mark is still visible, use a sand eraser or a small piece of fine-grit sandpaper.

Utility Knife

This is a good option for scraping away small unwanted burn marks in your design. Hold the utility knife securely and use the sharp point to gently scrape away the burn mark until fresh wood is revealed underneath. This erasing process does create small grooves in the wood depending on the size of the area you are removing. Using the technique in small areas will go unnoticed in the final artwork.

Sandpaper

This is a good option for lightening the color in a section of your design or removing burn marks completely. To lighten an area, rub the section lightly with 320-grit sandpaper until it reaches the desired color.

To erase an area completely, vigorously rub it with 80-grit sandpaper until the burn marks disappear. The rough-grit sandpaper will scratch the wood, so once the burn marks are removed, go over the area with 320-grit or higher sandpaper to smooth the wood surface. Use a dry cloth to wipe away any dust residue on the wood surface from the sanding. Hand sanding does require a fair amount of physical strength to rub fast and hard enough to erase the woodburning.

Electric Sander

This is a good option for erasing a large area of artwork or the entire woodburning with minimal effort. Erasing a design completely allows you to salvage the wood and start over. A random orbit electric hand sander will save you time because it gets the job done in a minute or so, depending on the size of the area you are erasing.

Start with 80-grit sandpaper to remove the woodburning from the targeted area. Then use 320-grit sandpaper or higher to smooth the wood surface. Use a dry cloth to wipe away any dust residue on the wood surface from the sanding.

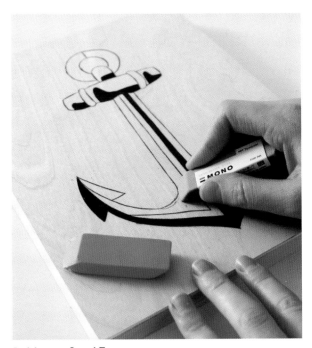

Rubber or Sand Eraser

Utility Knife

Sandpaper

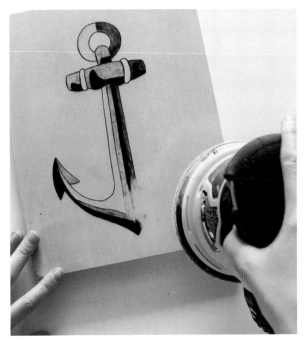

Electric Sander

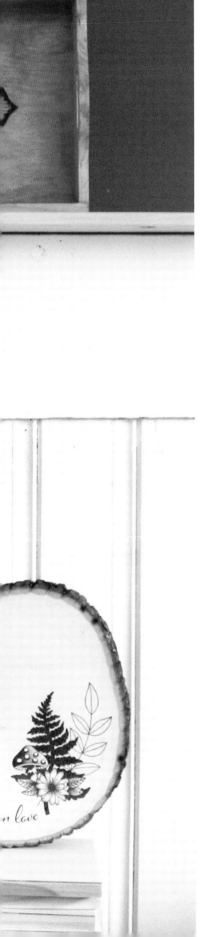

Projects

WELCOME TO THE PROJECT SECTION of the *Woodburning Workshop*!

Here we will explore and apply the woodburning techniques to create unique pieces of functional woodburning artwork on a variety of wooden items.

Follow along using the tool, nibs, and wood you have access to. When I say burn a straight line with the sharp edge of the universal nib, feel free to use your preferred nib to complete the straight line. Perhaps the rounded nib works better for you. When I say use a specific wooden item for a project, feel free to use any wooden item you would like to display the artwork on. When I say burn a specific pattern, feel free to make adjustments to the artwork by adding or subtracting elements to customize the art to your liking.

I am here to help guide you and give you inspiration for these ten woodburning projects. Nothing would make me happier than to see you as an artist take control of the tool, nibs, and wood you prefer to create artwork that represents and reflects who *you* are! Make your woodburning hobby and artwork unique to you.

Each project builds in difficulty and teaches you a brand-new skill. These skills are useful to learn so you can apply them to artwork outside of these ten projects. For example, learning how to shade petals on a flower to make them look three-dimensional or adding reflections in water will enhance your woodburning skills and personal artwork.

The most important thing is to have fun and let go of perfection. It can be intimidating to start a project, especially your very first project ever. Take a deep breath, believe in yourself, and burn!

You've got this! ❀

Welcome Sign

APPROXIMATE TIME: 2 HOURS

WELCOME TO THE FIRST PROJECT of the *Woodburning Workshop*! This welcome sign is a great candidate for your first woodburning project to gain confidence and insight into using your woodburning tool with step-by-step guidance. This project will teach you how to outline letters with straight and curved lines and fill in the letters with a crisscross shading pattern.

Find a piece of wood in your desired shape and size to create this beautiful, rustic sign. I used a rectangular piece of pine from my local craft store that included a twine strap and a sawtooth hook for hanging. If the wood you choose does not have a hook on the back, consider purchasing a small hook or twine to complete the last step of this project.

TOOLS & MATERIALS

- Woodburning tool
- Universal solid nib
- 20½" x 5" (52 x 12.5cm) wood piece
- Graphite paper
- Tape
- Pen or pencil
- Scissors
- Hook or twine
- Metal ruler (optional)
- Wood finish with application materials (optional)
- Pattern (pages 118–119)

STEP 1: Print the pattern. Copy the pattern on pages 118–119, resize it to fit the length of your wood piece, and print it out. Depending on the size of your wood, you may need to print the pattern over multiple pages and tape them together as described in Step 3: Print of Creating a Pattern (page 35). Center the printed pattern on the wood and tape down one edge.

STEP 2: Transfer the pattern. Slide a sheet of graphite paper under the pattern with the black carbon side facing down onto the wood. Trace the lines of the pattern with a pen or pencil. Be sure to trace all of the lines, including both lines outlining the letters.

STEP 3: Burn the letter outlines. Using the sharp edge of the universal solid nib on high heat, burn dark, thick lines to fill the space between the outlines of each letter. This burning technique will create the appearance of one large thick line that outlines each letter. Place the lines side-by-side with no space between them to fill the area completely. Burn slowly and apply lots of pressure. You can use the push or pull technique (page 38) for this step. Remember to adjust the position of the wood as you work, especially when burning curved sections, so you can always push or pull the nib toward or away from you easily.

TIP

If you want to fill your letters with perfectly straight lines, use a metal ruler to support and guide the nib while burning. Make sure your fingers aren't too close to the nib while burning or touching an area of the ruler that is hot from supporting the nib. Ouch!

STEP 4: Burn vertical lines. Use the sharp edge of the universal solid nib on high heat to burn thin, dark, vertical lines inside every other letter, starting with the W. Leave a small space between each line (the closer the lines are, the darker the shading effect will be). It is okay if the lines are not perfectly straight or spaced evenly. This will give the final art piece a rustic vibe! When you've finished adding lines to the W, move on to the L, O, and second E.

STEP 5: Burn horizontal lines. Follow the same technique to burn horizontal lines inside the letters from Step 4 (W, L, O, and second E). Adding these lines on top of the vertical lines creates a crisscross or checkerboard pattern for a unique shading effect. Keep the spacing of the horizontal lines the same as the spacing of the vertical lines in Step 4.

STEP 6: Burn diagonal lines. Follow the same technique to burn diagonal lines inside the remaining blank letters (the first E, C, and M). Burn the lines at a 45-degree angle to the letters, positioning them in the same direction. Use the same spacing you did in Steps 4 and 5.

Step 1

Step 2

Step 3

Step 4

Step 5

Step 6

STEP 7: Burn opposing diagonal lines. Now add diagonal lines going in the opposite direction to the same letters from Step 6 (the first E, C, and M). This creates a crisscross pattern with the lines running diagonally.

STEP 8: Burn the leaf and stem outlines. Use the sharp edge of the universal nib on high heat to burn the outlines of the leaves and stems. Notice how the thickness of the leaf outlines matches the thickness of the letter outlines. Use the same technique from Step 3 to fill the leaf outlines. The stem outlines are thin. Simply burn a dark line over the pattern line for the stems to outline them.

STEP 9: Burn a crisscross pattern in the stems. Add a crisscross pattern inside the stems. You can follow the technique in Steps 4 and 5 to burn the pattern vertically and horizontally, or follow the technique in Steps 6 and 7 to burn the pattern diagonally.

STEP 10: Seal the wood. This step is optional. If you like the raw wood look, you can keep your project unfinished as long as it remains indoors. If your sign will be placed outside, I recommend using a spar urethane finish to protect it from the elements and UV damage. An oil-based spar urethane will add a warm color to the wood grain, while a water-based one will go on clear. Follow the manufacturer's application and safety directions to apply your chosen finish.

STEP 11: Add a hanger. Once the finish is dry, add a small sawtooth hook or twine to the back of the sign. If adding twine, staple each end in place with a staple gun, or add a small nail to each end of the sign on the back and tie the ends of the twine onto them.

Step 7

Step 8

Step 9

Step 10

Step 11

Pine Tree Coasters

APPROXIMATE TIME: 1.5 HOURS FOR TWO COASTERS

THERE ISN'T A BETTER COMBINATION than woodburning a tree on a tree! I have discovered that combining nature images with wood canvases creates a relaxing nature-themed art environment. Spending a few hours focused on tree images while smelling the campfire scent from woodburning contributes significantly to a grounding and peaceful creative experience. If you close your eyes, you might even be able to imagine you are in a cozy mountain cabin, surrounded by forest and fresh air, enjoying a hot drink by a crackling fire while you woodburn your tree artwork. However, we will keep our eyes open for safety reasons! But do grab yourself a hot drink, and let's get started!

In this project, I'll show you how to create two different pine tree designs using two shading techniques with two different nibs. I used these designs to make coasters, but you can also turn them into ornaments (page 66). Before you get started, determine how many coasters or ornaments you'd like to make and which design you'd like to use so you can prepare your materials accordingly. You can burn both designs onto your coasters or choose your favorite one. For this project, use any round wood piece that is large enough to fit a coffee mug. Any type of wood will work. I found my unfinished wood rounds online.

TOOLS & MATERIALS

- ◆ Woodburning tool
- ◆ Universal solid nib
- ◆ Rounded solid nib
- ◆ 5" (12.5cm)-diameter wood rounds
- ◆ Graphite paper
- ◆ Tape

- ◆ Pen or pencil
- ◆ Scissors
- ◆ Wood finish with application materials
- ◆ Power drill and twine (optional)
- ◆ Patterns (pages 118–119)

STEP 1: Print the patterns. Copy the patterns on pages 118–119, resize them to fit your wood pieces, and print them out. Center the printed patterns on the wood pieces and tape down one edge.

STEP 2: Transfer the pattern. Slide a sheet of graphite paper under the patterns with the black carbon side facing down onto the wood. Trace the pattern lines with a pen or pencil, including those extending from the bottom of the tree branches. Trace the letter A or B as marked on each pattern to help identify the designs in the following steps.

STEP 3: Burn the outline of design A. Use the sharp edge of the universal solid nib on high heat to burn the curvy outline of the pine tree body and trunk. Burn all the lines extending from the bottoms of the branches. Use the push or pull technique (page 38) for this step, turning the wood as needed as you work.

STEP 4: Shade design A. Use the flat edge of the universal nib on high heat to shade the body of the tree and trunk with a solid dark burn. Strive for even shading that is as dark as possible (it should cover up the letter you traced in Step 2). I find it easiest to add shading by pulling my tool to the right (because I am right-handed) or down, depending on the section of the design I am burning. Use the top part of the flat edge only to burn shading in small areas, like the thin ends of the branches.

STEP 5: Burn more vertical lines. Use the sharp edge of the universal solid nib on high heat to add straight lines to the bottoms of the tree branches. Add one or two new lines between each of the existing lines. Make the new lines similar in length to the existing ones.

Step 1

Step 2

Step 3

Step 4

Step 5

STEP 6: Burn gradient shading. Use the flat edge of the universal solid nib on high heat to burn gradient shading on the bottoms of the tree branches. Apply heavy pressure where the vertical lines meet the bottom of the branch for a dark burn. Glide the nib down the vertical lines, reducing pressure as you go to make the burn gradually lighter. Finish the stroke at the bottom of the vertical lines. This should happen in one continuous motion.

STEP 7: Burn the outline of design B. Use the rounded solid nib on high heat to add dark dots along the outline of the pine tree and trunk. Place the dots close to one another with no space in between to cover up the graphite marks. Burn the small lines sticking out from the branches using rows of small dots. Your outline should have a slightly bumpy appearance, adding character and detail to the final silhouette.

STEP 8: Shade design B. Use the rounded solid nib on high heat to fill the tree with dark dots. Place the dots at random with no space between them. When finished, your tree will be filled with dark shading with a unique texture.

STEP 9: Seal the wood. Use a water-resistant, heat-resistant wood finish such as Danish oil to seal your coasters. This will keep them from warping or cracking due to heat or moisture. Danish oil has a matte finish and will make the wood grain color warmer and darker. If you're turning these pieces into ornaments, you can leave them unfinished or seal them with any wood finish you prefer.

OPTIONAL: Drill a hole for hanging. Once the finish is dry, you can drill a hole just above your pine tree to turn your finished piece into an ornament. Use a drill bit large enough to create a hole that will fit a piece of twine. Place a piece of scrap wood under your ornament and drill straight through the ornament into the scrap wood. Avoid drilling the hole too close to the top edge of the ornament to keep the wood from splitting.

OPTIONAL: Add twine. Thread a piece of twine or string through the hole and tie the ends together. If you having trouble pushing the thread through the hole, try using a sewing needle or safety pin to coax it through, or repeat the previous step to drill a slightly larger hole.

Step 6

Step 7

Step 8

Step 9

Optional

Optional

Rose Charcuterie Board

APPROXIMATE TIME: 3 HOURS

IT'S TIME TO LET YOUR INNER ARTIST BLOOM with this floral charcuterie board. If you don't have access to a charcuterie board, you can burn the rose design on any wood item or canvas of your choice. This project emphasizes the importance of shading to create realistic elements in woodburning artwork. You will burn dark to light gradient shading to add depth to the rose petals and leaves.

If your charcuterie board will be used for serving or displaying food, consider using a hardwood such as cherry, maple, walnut, or olive for your project. Hardwood is denser and less porous than softwood. It will withstand wear and tear from repetitive use and cleaning. I used a cherry charcuterie board that was hand-crafted by a local woodworker. If you can only find a softwood board such as pine, that's okay. Just be mindful of the type of food you serve on it. Avoid foods that are juicy or oily. Because softwoods absorb liquids, these foods can create stains on the board.

TOOLS & MATERIALS

- Woodburning tool
- Universal solid nib
- 15" x 8½" (38 x 21.5cm) charcuterie board with handle
- Graphite paper
- Tape
- Color pen
- Scissors
- Food-grade wood finish with application materials
- Pattern (page 120)

STEP 1: Print the pattern. Copy the pattern on page 120, resize it to fit your charcuterie board, and print it out. Place the printed pattern on the board where desired. You can put it in the center of the board or off to one side. Tape down one edge of the pattern.

STEP 2: Transfer the pattern. Slide a sheet of graphite paper under the pattern with the black carbon side facing down onto the wood. Trace the lines of the pattern, including the X's, with a colored pen. The colored pen will help you see where you have already traced and keep you from missing any lines. You do not need to make the bold lines of the rose thicker than the others. The extra thickness of these lines is simply a visual reference to guide the burning in the next step.

STEP 3: Burn the rose outline. Use the sharp edge of the universal solid nib on high heat to burn thick lines along all the rose petals. Refer to the pattern to determine which lines should be burned on thickly. Work slowly and with heavy pressure to burn lines about twice as thick as the graphite lines.

STEP 4: Burn the leaf outlines. Use the sharp edge of the universal solid nib on high heat to burn a thin dark line along the outline of the leaves and stems. Also burn the diagonal lines inside the leaves.

STEP 5: Burn the dark shading. Use the flat edge of the universal solid nib on high heat to burn dark shading in all the areas marked with an X. There are sections with X's in both the rose petals and the leaves. Refer to the pattern to ensure you didn't miss any of them. Use the top part of the flat edge only to burn shading in small, hard-to-reach areas.

Step 1

Step 2

Step 3

Step 4

Step 5

STEP 6: Burn the rose medium shading. Use the flat edge of the universal solid nib on medium heat to burn medium shading in all the areas shaded gray on the pattern. There are four small areas in the center of the rose. You want the finished shading to be a medium brown. Test your shading on a scrap piece of wood to know which temperature setting to use to create the ideal color.

STEP 7: Burn the rose gradient shading. Use the flat edge of the universal solid nib on medium heat to burn gradient shading inside each blank petal to add depth and realism to the rose. Apply heavy pressure at the base of each petal closest to the center of the rose for a medium burn. Glide the nib toward the outer edge of the petal, reducing pressure as you go to make the burn gradually lighter. The first third of the petal closest to the center should be a medium shade, the middle third of the petal should be a light shade, and the outer third of the petal should have no burning.

STEP 8: Burn the leaf stripes. Use the flat edge of the universal solid nib on high heat to add dark shading to the striped leaves. Burn dark shading in every other section of each leaf, starting at the base, to create a striped pattern.

STEP 9: Burn the leaf gradient shading. Use the flat edge of the universal nib on high heat to burn gradient shading in the remaining blank leaves. The shading should go from dark at the tip of each leaf to medium at the base where it touches the rose.

STEP 10: Burn the leaf stem shading. Use the flat edge of the universal nib on medium heat to burn medium shading in the two leaf stems where the stems meet the rose petals. This creates a shadow effect to show that the stems run underneath the rose petals.

STEP 11: Seal the wood. If you will use your charcuterie board to serve or display food, seal it with a food-grade wood finish. For my project, I applied mineral oil. Once dry, I added a beeswax wood finish on top for extra protection and sheen (optional). If you are not using food with your finished project, you can apply any wood finish of your choice.

BOARD CARE

Hand wash immediately after use with mild soap and warm water (*not dishwasher safe*). Do not submerge in water for long periods, as this will cause the wood to warp and crack. Towel dry after washing and then let air dry. Reapply food-grade wax or oil wood finish when you notice your board drying out, looking dull, or becoming lighter in color.

Step 6

Step 7

Step 8

Step 9

Step 10

Step 11

Projects: Rose Charcuterie Board

Butterfly with Watercolor

APPROXIMATE TIME: 2.5 HOURS

EVOLVE YOUR ARTISTRY and spread your creative wings by adding watercolor to this monarch butterfly design. Light, smooth woods like birch or basswood pair best with watercolor. The light color ensures the paint will remain vibrant, and the smooth surface allows the paint to blend, spread, and absorb with precision. If the wood you choose feels rough or coarse to the touch, use an electric hand sander to sand the surface with 320-grit sandpaper.

I used a light birch wood panel that I purchased from my local craft store. It was already sanded and very smooth, making it an ideal canvas for this project. I used inexpensive watercolor paints and a generic paintbrush. You don't need expensive or professional-grade materials to complete this project. Any brand of watercolor paint and brush will work great!

TOOLS & MATERIALS

- ◆ Woodburning tool
- ◆ Universal solid nib
- ◆ Rounded solid nib
- ◆ 8" x 10" (20.5 x 25.5cm) light wood canvas
- ◆ Graphite paper
- ◆ Tape
- ◆ Pen or pencil
- ◆ Scissors
- ◆ Red, orange, and yellow watercolor paint

- ◆ Paint tray
- ◆ Paintbrush
- ◆ Small cup of water
- ◆ Paper towel
- ◆ Wood finish with application materials (optional)
- ◆ Hook (optional)
- ◆ Pattern (page 121)

STEP 1: Print the pattern. Copy the pattern on page 121, resize it to fit your wood piece, and print it out. Center the printed pattern on the wood and tape down one edge.

STEP 2: Transfer the pattern. Slide a sheet of graphite paper under the pattern with the black carbon side facing down onto the wood. Trace the lines of the pattern, including the X's, with a pen or pencil. When tracing, you do not need to make the bold lines thicker than the others. These lines are simply a visual reference to guide the burning in the following steps.

STEP 3: Burn the butterfly outline. Use the sharp edge of the universal solid nib on high heat to burn the entire outer perimeter of the butterfly. This includes the wings, body, antennae, and legs, but not any of the shapes inside the butterfly.

STEP 4: Burn the interior shapes. Use the rounded solid nib on high heat to burn the outlines of all the circular and oval shapes inside the butterfly. It is okay if your burn lines are a little rough. You can smooth them out in the following steps. Just be sure they cover all the graphite marks.

STEP 5: Burn the dark shading. Use the flat edge of the universal solid nib on high heat to shade the entire body and wings of the butterfly as dark as possible. Follow the X's marked on the pattern to determine where you should add shading. Take your time to burn around and between all the circular and oval shapes.

STEP 6: Add the yellow watercolor. Refer to the pattern to identify the areas with bold outlines. These sections are where you'll add the watercolor. Apply yellow watercolor paint to the end of each shape closest to the butterfly's body (see Painting with Watercolor page 79). The paint should cover about one-third of the shape. If the color seems too dull, add more paint and less water to increase the color's vibrancy.

Step 1

Step 2

Step 3

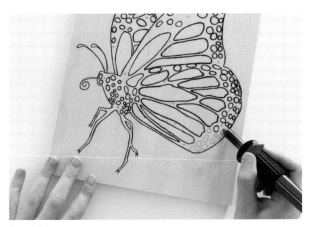

Step 4

Step 5

Step 6

STEP 7. Add the orange watercolor. Apply orange watercolor paint to the middle third of each shape. Be sure to gently blend the orange paint into the yellow paint as you add it. The two colors should blend seamlessly with some water, creating an ombre effect with the yellow transitioning into orange. If the orange watercolor seems too dull, add more paint and less water to increase the color's vibrancy.

STEP 8: Add the red watercolor. Apply red watercolor paint to the remaining third of each shape, blending it into the orange paint. The two colors should blend seamlessly, creating an ombre effect with the orange transitioning into the red. If the red watercolor seems too dull, add more paint and less water to increase the color's vibrancy.

STEP 9: Seal the wood. Seal your artwork only when your paint is dry to the touch. I used a spray-on, clear, semi-gloss, water-based interior polyurethane wood finish. It dries clear, does not darken the wood grain, and keeps the paint colors vibrant. I highly recommend using a spray-on water-based finish with watercolor to avoid smearing the paint during application. Note that any water-based finish can reactivate the watercolor paint, so you can also use an oil-based finish like tung or Danish oil. An oil-based finish may alter the paint colors slightly over time, adding a yellow hue to the paint and wood.

STEP 10: Add a hook. If you want to hang your art, add a hook or picture hanger to the back.

Step 7

Step 8

PAINTING WITH WATERCOLOR

Use any style of paintbrush that is proportionate to the size of your artwork (not too big and not too small). Wet the bristles in a small jar of water, shaking off any excess water gently. Run the wet paintbrush through the watercolor paint, mixing the water and paint on the brush and in the tray.

Apply the watercolor to the wood using small brushstrokes. If there is more water than paint on your brush, the color will be less vibrant, and the paint may spread across the wood surface into areas you didn't intend to paint. If there is more paint than water on your brush, the color will be more vibrant, and the paint will not spread very far across the wood.

Try to find the right mix of paint and water for your project so the color is vibrant, but the paint contains enough water to blend easily with other colors. You can practice on a scrap piece of wood to get the water/paint ratio on the brush just right. Use a dry cloth or cotton ball to clean up any paint or water drips that accidentally land on your woodburning design where you don't want them.

Step 9

Step 10

Birch Tree Hook Rack

APPROXIMATE TIME: 2.5 HOURS

BRANCH OUT IN YOUR WOODBURNING CREATIVITY by adding white acrylic paint to four rustic birch trees! This project will focus on burning gradient shading along one side of each tree to create a dimensional shadow effect. You will also learn how to add white acrylic paint to enhance the birch bark texture and make the trees pop out against the wood.

This project can serve as a stand-alone art piece, or you can make it functional by adding hooks. Please note that the project time listed above accounts for the woodburning and painting only. Additional time will be needed to allow the acrylic paint and wood finish to dry completely and to install hooks if desired.

I used a whimsical slab of cherry wood purchased from a local woodworker. It was run through a planer machine to make the wood surface level, and I sanded it using 320-grit sandpaper to smooth the surface. It is an inch thick, which gave me enough room to install hooks on the front using small screws. I suggest using a rectangular piece of wood for this project so you can burn and paint the birch trees across the length of the wood. Make sure your wood is thick enough to install the hooks of your choice.

TOOLS & MATERIALS

- ◆ Woodburning tool
- ◆ Universal solid nib
- ◆ Rounded solid nib
- ◆ 17½" x 8" (44.5 x 20.5cm) wood piece
- ◆ Graphite paper
- ◆ Tape
- ◆ Pen or pencil
- ◆ Scissors
- ◆ Metal ruler

- ◆ White acrylic paint
- ◆ Paintbrush
- ◆ Wood finish with application materials
- ◆ Two mounting hooks with installation tools for back
- ◆ Four hanging hooks with installation tools for front
- ◆ Pattern (page 122)

STEP 1: Print the pattern. Copy the pattern on page 122 and size it so the trees will reach from the top to the bottom of your wood piece. Print out the pattern. If you need more than four trees to cover your wood piece, you may need to print out multiple pattern pages. Cut out the trees and place them on your wood piece, using a ruler to space them out evenly. Tape down one edge of each tree.

STEP 2: Transfer the pattern. Slide a sheet of graphite paper under the pattern with the black carbon side facing down onto the wood. Trace the lines of the pattern, including the X's, with a pen or pencil. Repeat for each tree.

STEP 3: Burn the outlines. Use the sharp edge of the universal solid nib on high heat to burn bold outlines along all the traced lines. Burn slowly and apply heavy pressure to create lines twice as thick as the graphite lines. These thick lines will be easier to paint around in the following steps.

STEP 4: Burn the dark shading. Use the rounded solid nib on high heat to burn dark shading in all the areas marked with an X. Use the swirl technique (page 48) to create dark, textured shading. Burn slowly and with heavy pressure, overlapping the random swirls and squiggles to fill each area. Fill in all the small unmarked circle shapes in the bark as well.

STEP 5: Burn the dark shadows. Use the flat edge of the universal solid nib on high heat to burn a solid black shadow along the left side of each trunk and branch. Each shadow should cover about one-quarter of the corresponding trunk or branch. Burning the shadows will cover some of the outlines you burned in Step 3. This is okay.

STEP 6: Burn the gradient shading. Use the flat edge of the universal solid nib on medium heat to burn gradient shading on the left side of each tree and branch. Apply heavy pressure at the edge of each shadow for a medium burn. Glide the nib toward the center of the tree, reducing pressure as you go to make the burn gradually lighter. You do not have to line up your burn marks so they all end in exactly the same place. Also, the color of the shading does not have to match exactly. This will give your tree a more realistic look.

TIP

Because I am right-handed, my gradient shading instructions apply to right-handers. If you are left-handed, it will be easier to start the gradient shading on the right side of the tree trunk and pull your tool to the left. Feel free to adapt my instructions accordingly, adding shading to the right sides of the trees and paint to the left sides.

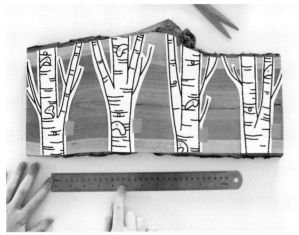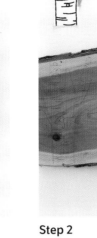

Step 1

Step 2

Step 3

Step 4

Step 5

Step 6

STEP 7: Add the white acrylic paint. Use a small paintbrush to paint a solid white section along the right side of each trunk and branch. The paint should cover about one-quarter of each trunk and branch. Avoid painting directly over any burn lines. If you get paint on a burn line, use a toothpick to scratch it off lightly.

STEP 8: Paint the bark texture. Make small horizontal brush strokes on each trunk and branch. Each stroke should start in the white painted area you added in the previous step and move toward the center of the trunk or branch. This technique is similar to adding the gradient shading. The strokes should vary slightly in length and thickness and overlap to create a realistic texture. Avoid painting directly over any burn lines. However, it is okay if some of the paint extends onto the gradient shading.

STEP 9: Seal the wood. Allow the paint to dry for at least 24 hours, then apply a wood finish to protect your project from chips and scratches. I used a water-based, clear, semi-gloss polycrylic. It dries clear and does not alter the color of the paint like some oil-based wood finishes do. You can also use water-based polyurethane for a clear finish.

STEP 10: Add hooks on the back. Once the wood finish is dry, install two mounting hooks on either end of the wood on the back side. Make sure they are level so your project will hang straight.

STEP 11: Add hooks on the front. Install any size and style hooks you'd like to the front of the wood. I used four small matte black hooks to match the black woodburning in the art and blend into the trees. You can install your hooks between each tree or on each tree near the bottom edge of the wood.

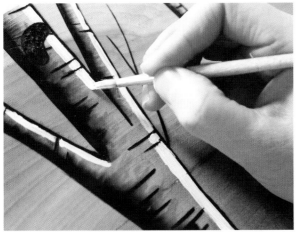

Step 7

Step 8

Step 9

Step 10

Step 11

Utensil Set

APPROXIMATE TIME: 2 HOURS

IT'S THYME TO MIX IT UP and challenge yourself by woodburning on the uneven surfaces of wooden utensils! The utensils may be wobbly or slippery on your work surface due to their light weight and round handles, so for extra grip, place them on a small non-slip mat while you work. This project will require a steady hand and lots of focus to burn along the pattern outlines.

I used three acacia wood utensils with no finish purchased from a kitchen supply store. Their surface is super smooth and ready to burn. If the utensils you choose have a rough surface, hand sand or use an electric hand sander to smooth the surfaces using 320-grit sandpaper. Use a dry cloth to wipe off any dust after sanding.

I hope this project inspires you to woodburn more utensil sets using your own custom words, names, and designs to create a set for yourself or a personalized gift for someone else. I gifted my sister a mushroom-themed utensil set because she loves mushrooms and baking. I used the "mix it" pattern and added "our favorite baker" to another handle and simple mushroom designs on the heads of the spoon and spatulas. You can get really creative with wooden utensils!

TOOLS & MATERIALS

- ◆ Woodburning tool
- ◆ Universal solid nib
- ◆ Rounded solid nib
- ◆ 3 wooden utensils (spoon, slotted spatula, spatula)
- ◆ Graphite paper
- ◆ Tape

- ◆ Pen and pencil
- ◆ Scissors
- ◆ Metal ruler (optional)
- ◆ Wood finish with application materials
- ◆ Non-slip mat (optional)
- ◆ Pattern (page 123)

STEP 1: Print and trace the pattern. Copy the Mix It pattern on page 123, resize it to fit your wooden spoon's handle, and print it out. Center the printed pattern on the spoon's handle and tape down one edge. Slide a sheet of graphite paper under the pattern with the black carbon side facing down onto the wood. Trace the lines of the pattern with a pen or pencil.

STEP 2: Burn the lettering. Slide a non-slip mat under the spoon to keep it in place while you work. Use the rounded solid nib on high heat to burn the words with bold lines. Make sure all the letters are equally thick. Hold the spoon tightly with your free hand to keep it in place. Be sure your fingers do not get too close to the hot nib.

STEP 3: Shade the spoon head. Use the rounded solid nib on high heat to burn dark dots along the border of the spoon head. Next, fill in the rest of the spoon head with large dark dots placed with no space between them. This creates a unique dark textured pattern.

STEP 4: Draw diagonal lines. With a ruler and pencil, draw diagonal lines at a 45-degree angle across the slotted spatula. Cover the entire length of the spatula, spacing the lines about a ruler's width apart. If you don't have access to a ruler or your spatula handle is rounded, you can draw on the lines by hand.

STEP 5: Draw leaves. Use a pencil to draw leaf pairs of various sizes along the diagonal lines. Space each pair of leaves about half an inch apart.

Step 1

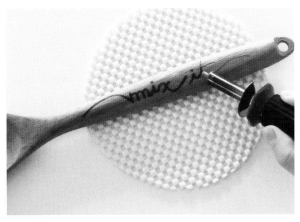

Step 2

Step 3

Step 4

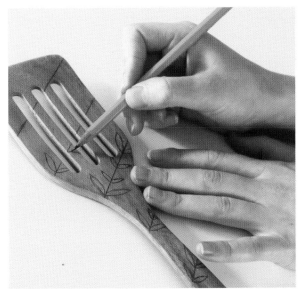

Step 5

STEP 6: Burn the vine. Slide a non-slip mat under the spatula. Use the sharp edge of the universal solid nib on high heat to burn the diagonal lines twice as thick as the pencil lines. If desired, burn the lines so they wrap around the edges of the spatula toward the back. Use the sharp edge of the nib to burn the outlines of the leaves, then use the flat edge to burn dark shading inside the leaves.

STEP 7: Print and trace the pattern. Copy the herb pattern on page 123, resize it to fit the remaining spatula's head, and print it out. Center the printed pattern on the spatula's head and tape down one edge. Transfer the pattern onto the spatula using graphite paper.

STEP 8: Burn the lettering. Slide a non-slip mat under the spatula. Use the rounded solid nib on high heat to burn the cursive writing. Make the burned lines slightly thicker than the graphite marks. The lettering will appear bolder than the herb artwork burned in the next step.

STEP 9: Burn the herbs. Use the sharp edge of the universal solid nib on high heat to burn the outlines of the herbs with thin dark lines. Take your time and move the spatula around on the non-slip mat as you burn the fine details.

STEP 10: Finish the wood. Apply food-grade mineral oil to the utensils with a clean cloth and set them aside to dry. Once the finish is dry, the utensil set is ready to use!

UTENSIL CARE

Hand-wash only in warm water with mild soap immediately after use (*not dishwasher safe*). Never submerge or let your utensils sit in water for long periods, as this will cause the wood to warp and crack. Let air dry. Reapply mineral oil when you notice the wood is drying out, looking dull, or becoming lighter in color.

Step 6

Step 7

Step 8

Step 9

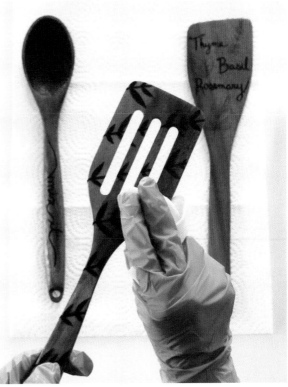

Step 10

Wedding Centerpiece

APPROXIMATE TIME: 3 HOURS

YOU WILL FALL IN LOVE with this project as you grow your woodburning skillset. You'll burn the entire design using only a rounded or ball-point nib. Burning with a rounded nib requires a steady hand and even pressure to precisely burn uniform lines. When burning with a round nib, a thin line is created when a small fraction of the nib's surface contacts the wood. A thick line is created when a large portion of the nib's surface contacts the wood. The more pressure you apply as you are burning, the thicker the line will be. Shading color depends on the nib's temperature and your woodburning technique. Remember to burn slowly and take your time with this project.

Use any large circular or oval slice of wood so the artwork can curve along the wood's edge. I used a large basswood round I found at my local craft store. Once you've completed this project, you will have a stunning earthy centerpiece for a wedding, your home, or to gift to an outdoorsy couple!

TOOLS & MATERIALS

- Woodburning tool
- Ball stylus fixed-tip pen or any rounded nib
- 12½" (32cm)-diameter round wood slice
- Graphite paper
- Tape
- Pen or pencil
- Scissors
- Wood finish with application materials (optional)
- Pattern (page 124)

STEP 1: Print the pattern. Copy the pattern on page 124, resize it to fit your wood piece, and print it out. Position the printed pattern along the edge of the wood piece and tape down one edge.

STEP 2: Transfer the pattern. Slide a sheet of graphite paper under the pattern with the black carbon side facing down onto the wood. Trace the outline of each letter and all the lines in the bouquet artwork, including the X's and DT's, with a pen or pencil. As before, the X's mark areas that require dark shading. The DT's mark areas that require dotted shading. Do not trace any of the gray shading onto the wood. This is simply a visual reference to guide the burning in the following steps.

STEP 3: Burn the letters. Use the ball stylus fixed-tip pen on high heat to burn the lettering. You can skip burning the letter outlines and jump right into burning dark shading and lines. Burn directly within the traced lines to shade. Each letter has thick and thin lines. Apply heavy pressure to burn thick lines. Use light pressure and consistent motion to burn thin lines. As the lines of each letter transition from thin to thick and vice versa, you will need to adjust the pressure you use accordingly.

STEP 4: Burn the plant outlines. Use the ball stylus fixed-tip pen on high heat to burn the outlines of the plants. Do your best to keep the burn lines smooth and equal in thickness.

STEP 5: Burn dots. Use the ball stylus fixed-tip pen on high heat to burn dark dots deep into all the areas labeled with DT. Burn dots along the edges of each section first, and then fill the center. Burn each dot at random with no specific pattern, placed closely together to fill the entire space. Each dot should take about one to two seconds to burn. The result will be a dark and textured burn pattern.

TIP

Depending on the size and shape of your wood piece, the curve of the elements in the pattern may not match the curve of the wood's edge. If so, in Step 1, cut out each individual word and the plant artwork separately. Place the cutouts along the edge of your word piece, matching the curve of the edge. Tape down one edge of each cutout for tracing.

Step 1

Step 2

Step 3

Step 4

Step 5

STEP 6: Burn the dark shading. Use the ball stylus fixed-tip pen on high heat to burn all the areas marked with an X with dark shading. Burn thin dark vertical lines side by side to create the shading, making a textured stripe pattern.

STEP 7: Burn the dark shadows. Use the ball stylus fixed-tip pen on high heat to burn one thick curved line along the bottom half of each small circle in the mushroom cap. Burn only along the outer perimeter of each circle to create a shadow effect.

STEP 8: Burn the gradient shading in the mushroom. Use the ball stylus fixed-tip pen to burn gradient shading across the mushroom cap. Burn the shading using horizontal lines. Start with high heat to burn dark lines on the left side of the cap, extending across about one-third of the cap. Use medium heat to burn medium shading across the next third of the cap. Use low heat to burn light shading across the final third of the cap along the right side. Avoid adding shading to the dots on the cap.

STEP 9: Burn medium shading in the flower petals. Use the ball stylus fixed-tip pen on medium heat to burn medium shading in all the areas shaded gray on the pattern. Burn the shading using side-by-side lines that follow the direction of each petal.

STEP 10: Burn gradient shading in the leaves. Use the ball stylus fixed-tip pen to burn gradient shading in the four leaves of the flower. Burn the shading using random overlapping swirls and squiggles. Start with high heat to burn dark shading in the third of the leaves closest to the petals. Use medium heat to burn medium shading in the next third of the leaves. Use low heat to burn light shading in the final third of the leaves. The finished shading should look rustic and rigid.

STEP 11: Seal the wood. You can leave this project natural or apply a finish. Avoid using a wood stain to keep the shading from getting lost in the stain color. It is best to use a food-grade finish, Danish oil, or a clear water-based polyurethane finish to keep the woodburning artwork vibrant.

Step 6

Step 7

Step 8

Step 9

Step 10

Projects: Wedding Centerpiece

Nature Box

APPROXIMATE TIME: 2 HOURS

LET THIS NATURE LANDSCAPE ARTWORK REFLECT the true woodburning artist that you are! This project will focus on creating realistic reflections in the water using a variety of shading styles and wavy line details. The water quickly becomes the focal point of the artwork, while the other design components include silhouettes and simple details. There are a few large areas that require dark shading. To speed up shading these large areas, you can use a micro-jet torch to quickly fill in the spaces.

Use a box with no wood finish for this project and burn the artwork directly onto the lid. Craft stores have a variety of unfinished wooden boxes in many shapes and styles. Once you've completed burning the lid, you can burn the box sides, inside the lid, and the base inside the box with any designs or words of your choice. One suggestion is to use the other woodburning patterns from this book, such as the pine trees, birch trees, or owl, to burn the rest of the box.

If you don't have access to a plain wooden box for this project, you can use any rectangular piece of wood and create a nature scene!

TOOLS & MATERIALS

- ◆ Woodburning tool
- ◆ Universal solid nib
- ◆ Micro-jet torch (optional)
- ◆ 8½" x 5½" (21.5 x 14cm) wooden box
- ◆ Graphite paper
- ◆ Tape
- ◆ Pen or pencil
- ◆ Scissors
- ◆ Wood finish with application materials
- ◆ Household item with a similar height to your box
- ◆ Non-slip mat
- ◆ Pattern (page 125)

STEP 1: Print the pattern. Copy the pattern on page 125 and resize it to fit your box. Your box may have different dimensions than mine. Resize the pattern so it is slightly larger than your box, then crop it to fit the lid of your box. Print out the pattern. Position it on the box lid and tape down one edge.

STEP 2: Transfer the pattern. Slide a sheet of graphite paper under the pattern with the black carbon side facing down onto the wood. Trace the lines of the pattern, including the X's, with a pen or pencil. Use a household item that has a similar height to your box to rest your hand on. I used an upside-down plant pot on a non-slip mat.

STEP 3: Burn the outline. Use the sharp edge of the universal solid nib on high heat to outline the design with dark lines. The artwork should stretch across the entire surface of the lid, so extend any lines that do not reach the edge of the lid so that they do. I had to slightly extend and burn all the lines around the perimeter of the design to meet the lid edges, such as the trees, mountains, and land outlines.

STEP 4: Burn the dark shading. Use the flat edge of the universal solid nib on high heat to burn dark shading in all the areas marked with an X. Some areas are quite large and will require some time to burn. To speed up the shading process, use a micro-jet torch to burn large areas in seconds. Hold the torch a few inches away from the wood and use it to burn the centers of the large areas. Then use your universal solid nib to fill in the rest of the space. Feel free to use the micro-jet torch on a scrap piece of wood to learn the flame's size and practice before burning your box lid.

STEP 5: Burn the grass and tree details. Use the sharp edge of the universal solid nib on high heat to burn grass details along the edge of the land silhouette where the four fern plants are located. Burn small lines coming up from the silhouette's edge. Make them dark and thin of varying lengths, but no longer than halfway up the fern plants. Each line should vary in direction, some going straight up and others to the right or left. Next, burn tiny, dark, closely-packed lines extending straight up from the thick black strip along the bottom of the mountain range. These tiny lines should resemble a row of tiny pine trees in the distance along the bottom of the mountain.

TIP

Use any household item that has a similar height to your box, such as an upsidedown mug or plant pot, to rest your hand on. This is helpful for tracing and burning any piece of wood that sits high off your work surface. You will have better hand control and accuracy when burning areas of the wood where you cannot rest your hand on the table.

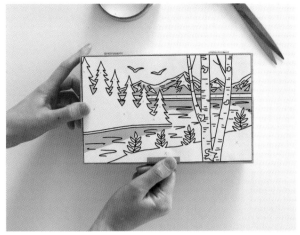

Step 1

Step 2

Step 4

Step 3

Step 5

STEP 6: Burn the medium shading. Use the flat edge of the universal solid nib on medium heat to burn medium shading in all the areas of the mountains shaded gray on the pattern. The shading should have an even color and cover the area from the bottom of the mountain almost to the top, leaving an untouched border along the top edge. We will shade the gray areas under the mountain range and large trees in Step 8.

STEP 7: Burn the light shading. Use the flat edge of the universal solid nib on low heat to burn thick, straight, horizontal lines at random across the water. The burn marks should be light, but dark enough to show through any wood finish. Make the lines varying lengths. Burn lines between and across the dark squiggle outlines on the water to create a wave effect. You can always add more lines after you have completed the rest of the steps if you decide your water needs more.

STEP 8: Burn the gradient shading. Use the flat edge of the universal solid nib on high heat to burn gradient shading in all the areas below the mountains and large pine trees shaded gray on the pattern. Start with heavy pressure along the shoreline for a dark burn. Glide the nib down toward the bottom edge of the lid, reducing pressure as you go to make the burn gradually lighter. The shading should end where the gray area on the pattern does. It is okay to burn over some of the horizontal lines in Step 7 and the outlines from Step 3.

STEP 9: Burn the dark shading. Use the flat edge of the universal solid nib on high heat to burn dark shading in the water under each large pine tree (six in total). Start under a tree near the shoreline in the dark shading area. Pull the nib straight down, ending just before the grass details. Burn the shading in narrow triangles to match the shape of the trees.

STEP 10: Seal the wood. I used tung oil to seal my box. Tung oil darkens the wood grain to create a rustic finish but preserves the light shading in the water. Be sure you are finished burning, including the sides and inside of the box, before applying any finish. Feel free to use any wood finish you have on hand.

Step 6

Step 7

Step 8

Step 9

Step 10

Owl Artwork

APPROXIMATE TIME: 3 HOURS

THIS PROJECT IS GOING TO BE A HOOT! At first glance, this realistic great horned owl design may look intimidating, but this project uses only fundamental techniques learned throughout this book. When we break down the realistic owl image into categories of lines, dots, and shading, woodburning this design quickly becomes achievable. I suggest sizing this owl at least as large as your hand to ensure you can accurately transfer all the intricate pattern lines and woodburn the small details.

The longest but most important steps of this project are transferring and woodburning the outline. Once the outline is burned with precision, the rest of the steps will be easier to complete. So don't rush completing the outline, even if it feels like it takes you a long time.

I used a medium-size wood round with bark that I found at my local craft store. I sanded the surface using an electric hand sander with 320-grit sandpaper. Most wood products at craft stores are already smooth, but I still like to sand mine to get the smoothest surface possible. Avoid using wood with a strong grain pattern, such as pine. The grain pattern and softness of pine wood make it difficult to burn with accuracy and intricacy. Aim for a light-colored wood such as basswood or birch for this project.

Achieving realistic woodburning artwork is more dependent on having a smooth surface on high-quality wood than using an expensive professional-grade woodburning tool. A smooth surface is more receptive to the heat of your nib and your woodburning techniques so you can burn with accuracy and precision.

TOOLS & MATERIALS

- ◆ Woodburning tool
- ◆ Universal solid nib
- ◆ Rounded solid nib
- ◆ 8" (20.5cm)-diameter wood round
- ◆ Graphite paper
- ◆ Tape
- ◆ Color pen
- ◆ Scissors
- ◆ Wood finish with application materials (optional)
- ◆ Hook (optional)
- ◆ Pattern (page 126)

STEP 1: Print the pattern. Copy the pattern on page 126, resize it to fit your wood piece, and print it out. It is difficult to trace or burn details smaller than the tip of your pen or nib, so I suggest making this design at least as large as your hand. Center the printed pattern on the wood and tape down one edge.

STEP 2: Transfer the pattern. Slide a sheet of graphite paper under the pattern with the black carbon side facing down onto the wood. Trace the lines of the pattern, including the X's, with a color pen. Some of the X's may be too small to trace. In this case, you can use the printed pattern for reference in the following steps. Do not trace the outline of the gray areas. These are only a visual reference for the following steps. If your wood has knots like the one in the center of mine, place the pattern to incorporate the knots in the darker areas of the artwork.

STEP 3: Burn the outline. Use the sharp edge of the universal solid nib on high heat to burn thin, dark lines over every outline of the pattern. This step is time-consuming, but once you are finished burning the outline, you are more than halfway finished with the project in terms of time. The rest of the steps are fairly quick! So go slow and burn every outline with precision.

STEP 4: Burn the dark features. Use the flat edge of the universal solid nib on high heat to burn dark shading in all the areas marked with an X. Refer to your printed pattern to catch any areas with X's that you may not have been able to transfer to the wood.

STEP 5: Burn the medium shading. Use the flat edge of the universal solid nib on medium heat to burn medium shading in all the areas shaded gray on the pattern—the ears, arches along the forehead, at the top of the eyeballs, along the top of the beak on both sides, the cheeks, and within the circle on the beak.

STEP 6: Burn the gradient shading. Use the flat edge of the universal solid nib on high heat to burn gradient shading on the belly of the owl. Start with heavy pressure on one of the dark spots on the owl's belly for a dark burn. Glide the nib down toward the bottom of the design, reducing pressure as you go to make the burn gradually lighter, ending with a light color. These should be short burn marks, but vary the length to create a realistic feathery look. Continue to burn gradient shading on all the large dark spots on the belly.

Step 1

Step 2

Step 3

Step 4

Step 5

Step 6

STEP 7: Burn a crisscross pattern. Use the sharp edge of the universal solid nib on high heat to create a crisscross pattern of thin dark lines over the entire area of medium shading on the owl's cheeks. Extend the lines a tiny bit over the dark shaded area that runs vertically along both sides of the cheeks. Burn the crisscross pattern using diagonal lines going in opposite directions.

STEP 8: Burn horizontal line details. Use the sharp edge of the universal solid nib on high heat to burn horizontal lines across the owl's forehead. The lines should be slightly curved to match the arch of the owl's head. There is no right or wrong placement for these lines. Burn them at random, and feel free to place them directly over top of any other previously burned areas on the forehead.

STEP 9: Burn the feather details. Use the sharp edge of the universal solid nib on high heat to burn thin lines in the ears, underneath the eyes, and on the belly (see Burning Fur or Feather Detail page 50). Keep the lines thin but dark so they are visible, and vary them in length and direction. Space each line far apart like I did to create a light, feathery look. Burn feather lines in the ears directly over the areas of medium shading, pointing toward the top of the design. Burn feather lines under the eyes in the areas of medium shading with dark blotches, extending down toward the crisscross areas. Burn feather lines on the belly along the bottom of the neck, extending down toward the bottom of the design.

STEP 10: Burn the dot details. Use the rounded solid nib on high heat to add rows of small dark dots on the forehead. Each row should include two to four dots. Like Step 8, burn these rows randomly across the owl's forehead. They can be burned over previously burned areas. Burn clusters of dots throughout the belly around the dark blotches. Each cluster should include five to ten dots.

STEP 11: Seal the wood. If your owl artwork will be used for wall art only and you prefer the look of raw wood, it is perfectly okay to keep your project unfinished as long as you keep it out of direct sunlight. UV exposure will fade the artwork and wood over time. I suggest a clear polyurethane wood finish if you prefer to seal your wood. This finish dries clear and does not alter the wood grain color, preserving the artwork's integrity, contrast, and vibrancy.

STEP 12: Add a hook. If you want to hang your art, add a hook or picture hanger to the back.

Step 7

Step 8

Step 9

Step 10

Step 11

Step 12

Multi-Purpose Mandala Tray

APPROXIMATE TIME: 3 HOURS

MANDALA ART IS A MINDFUL PRACTICE to relax, enhance creativity, and increase your focus. Combine mandala art with the slow nature of woodburning, and you have yourself an extraordinary experience of cultivating inner peace and awareness.

For this project, I used a sharp-edge fixed-tip pen, shading bowl fixed-tip pen, and ball stylus fixed-tip pen, but feel free to use any woodburning tool, pens, and nibs available to you. The final results will be the same no matter what tools you use, as long as you follow the pattern. Choose a wooden tray, such as the basswood one I used, or choose any wood product you prefer. Mandalas are a great woodburning addition to any wood item or canvas.

This project will elevate your creativity by encouraging you to burn shading and details with little guidance from the pattern. Reuse this mandala pattern repeatedly to burn new mandalas using different burn patterns, details, and shading each time. You can position your mandala in the center of your wood, off to the side, or even burn multiple mandalas on one piece of wood. The creative possibilities are endless with this project. I suggest burning the center of each mandala first and working your way outward, adding details and shading.

TOOLS & MATERIALS

- ◆ Woodburning tool
- ◆ Sharp-edge nib
- ◆ Shading nib
- ◆ Ball stylus or rounded nib
- ◆ 15" x 11" (38 x 28cm) wooden tray
- ◆ Graphite paper
- ◆ Tape
- ◆ Pen or pencil
- ◆ Scissors
- ◆ Wood finish with application materials
- ◆ Pattern (page 127)

STEP 1: Print the pattern. Copy the pattern on page 127, resize it to fit your wood tray, and print it out. Place the printed pattern on the tray where desired and tape down one edge.

STEP 2: Transfer the pattern. Slide a sheet of graphite paper under the pattern with the black carbon side facing down onto the wood. Trace the lines of the pattern with a pen or pencil.

STEP 3: Burn the outline. Use the sharp-edge fixed-tip pen on high heat to burn the outline of the mandala. Take your time along all the curved lines to create a thin, clean outline. The outlines can be thick or thin or a mix of both. I burned a uniform line throughout my mandala. For the tight curves, I roll my pen between my fingers to twist the knife edge along the pattern line.

STEP 4: Burn the dark shading. Use the shading bowl fixed-tip pen on high heat to burn dark shading in the innermost circle of the mandala and the area around the four small petal outlines.

STEP 5: Burn dots. Use the ball stylus fixed-tip pen on high heat to add one large dot in each of the four larger semicircles and one small dot in each of the small semicircles around the mandala's center.

STEP 6: Burn a leaf pattern. Use the sharp-edge fixed-tip pen on high heat to burn one straight line up the center of each tall leaf (eight in total). On both sides of the straight line, burn four smaller lines extending up on a diagonal toward the outer edge of the leaf. Space these lines evenly apart.

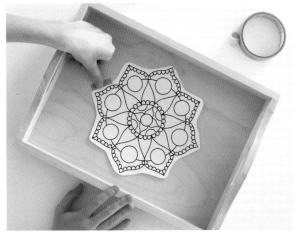

Step 1

Step 2

Step 3

Step 4

Step 5

Step 6

Projects: Multi-Purpose Mandala Tray

STEP 7: Burn the dark shading. Use the shading bowl fixed-tip pen on high heat to burn dark shading in the space around the eight leaves.

STEP 8: Burn the dark circles. Use the shading bowl fixed-tip pen on medium heat to burn a light circle outline within each of the circles. Add a crescent moon shape in the top left area of each circle. Turn the tool to high heat and fill the circle with dark shading, leaving the crescent moon blank to create a three-dimensional effect.

STEP 9: Burn a dark border. Use the shading bowl fixed-tip pen on high heat to burn dark shading in each semicircle along the outermost edge of the mandala.

STEP 10: Burn lines along the arches. Use the sharp-edge fixed-tip pen on high heat to burn thin straight lines radiating out from each circle to the outer edge of the mandala. Space the lines evenly.

STEP 11: Seal the wood. If your tray will be used for non-food items like books or candles, seal it using any finish available to you to protect it from repetitive wear and tear. If you will serve food directly on the tray, seal the wood with a food-grade wood finish such as mineral oil. I used an oil-based finish in an oak color for a durable finish and a rich stain color that is not too dark.

Step 7

Step 8

Step 9

Step 10

Step 11

fall in love grow in love

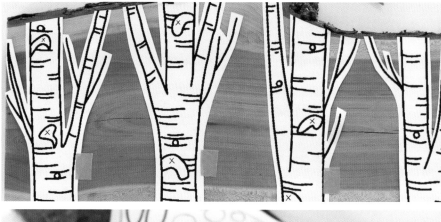

Patterns

HERE YOU WILL FIND ALL OF THE PATTERNS needed to create the projects in this book. Remember, depending on what is available to you or your personal preference, you may use wood pieces that are larger or smaller than the ones I used to create the projects in this book. Any of the patterns can be resized to fit the wood canvas of your choosing, see the guidance on printing your pattern (page 35).

In addition to changing the size of the patterns, you can always adapt these designs to better match your unique style. Remove or add elements, change the words to something meaningful to you, or mix and match elements of different designs to create an entirely new pattern. Have fun and be creative! ❁

Downloadable Patterns

You can download and print the full-sized patterns for these woodburning projects at http://tinyurl.com/11493-patterns-download.

ACCESSING AND USING THE PATTERNS

To access a pattern through the tiny url, type the web address provided into your browser window.

Print directly from the browser window or download the pattern.

To print at home, print the letter-size pages, selecting 100% size on the printer. Use dashed/dotted lines to trim, layer, and tape together pages as needed.

To print at a copyshop, save the full-size pages to a thumb drive or email them to your local copyshop for printing.

Welcome Sign, instructions on page 56

*(Copy at 120% for a 20½" x 5" (52 x 12.5cm) wood piece,
copying each half of pattern and piecing together between O & M)*

Pine Tree Coasters, instructions on page 62

(Copy at 100% for 5" (12.5cm)-diameter wood rounds)

Pine Tree Coasters, instructions on page 62

(Copy at 100% for 5" (12.5cm)-diameter wood rounds)

Patterns

Rose Charcuterie Board,
instructions on page 68

(Copy at 100% for a
15" x 8½" (38 x 21.5cm) wood board)

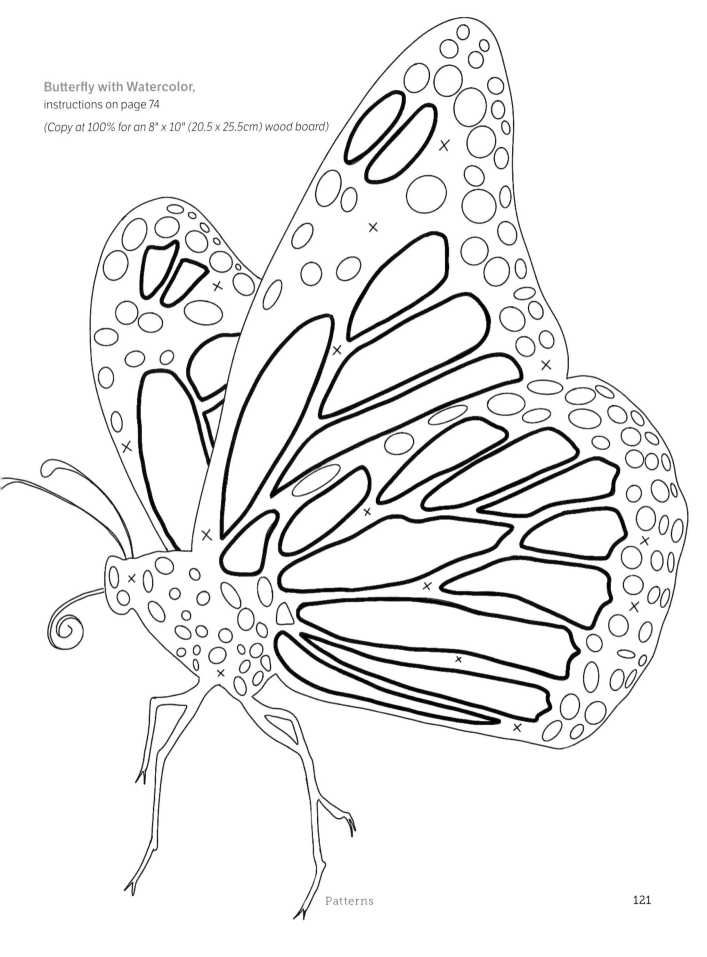

Butterfly with Watercolor,
instructions on page 74

(Copy at 100% for an 8" x 10" (20.5 x 25.5cm) wood board)

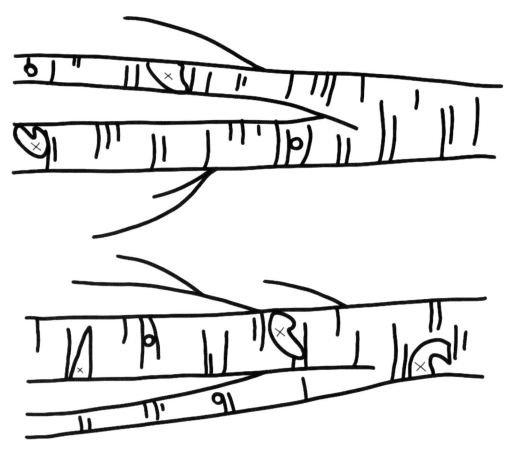

Birch Tree Hook Rack, instructions on page 80

(Copy at 200% for a 17½" x 8" (44.5 x 20.5cm) wood piece)

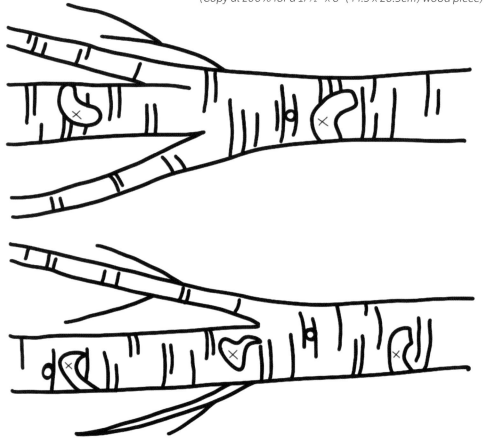

Utensil Set, instructions on page 86

(Copy at 100% for a 13" (33cm) wooden spatula and a 12" (30.5cm) wooden spoon)

Fall in love, grow in love

Wedding Centerpiece, instructions on page 92

(Copy at 115% for a 12½" (32cm)-diameter round wood slice)

Nature Box, instructions on page 98

(Copy at 100% for a 8½" x 5½" (21.5 x 14cm) wooden box)

Owl Artwork,
instructions on page 104

*(Copy at 100% for an
8" (20.5cm)-diameter wood round)*

Woodburning Workshop

Multi-Purpose Mandala Tray,
instructions on page 110

(Copy at 110% for a 15" x 11" (38 x 28cm) wooden tray)